BROWN MULE 7

Life of a 5th Battalion, 7th Cavalry Combat Wireman in Vietnam 1966-1967

Written by Mike Toyne, as told through Leon Toyne's Vietnam Letters

All rights reserved.

First published and printed in the United States of America. No Part of this book may be used or reproduced in any manner whatsoever without written permission except in the case of brief quotations embodied in critical articles and reviews.

For information, address **Book Writing Cube**
651 Broad St #206 Middleton, DE 19709

302-883-8877

https://www.bookwritingcube.com/

Published by **Book Writing Cube**

Printed in the United States

Copyright (c) 2023 by Mike Toyne

Page left blank for Publication

DISCLAIMER

BROWN MULE 7

Life of a 5th Battalion, 7th Cavalry Combat Wireman in Vietnam 1966-1967

Copyright ©2023 Michael Toyne

Full-Color Hardcover ISBN: 9798376560938

Black and White Paperback ISBN: 9780578279947

E-Book ASIN: B0BV9BZC6M

All rights reserved. No part of this book may be reproduced in any form or by any means, electronic, mechanical, photocopying, recording, or otherwise, without the author's written permission, except for a reviewer, who may quote a brief passage in a review.

The author does not claim copyright to the photos in this work, as they were obtained from various sources but requests that, if used, proper credit be given to the original owner, as noted in the caption. Unless otherwise noted in the caption, all photos must be assumed to have been contributed by Leon Toyne, Steve Vincent, Frank Farrell, Steve Streeter, Will Bowe, or the subject of the photo.

Every effort has been made to trace copyright holders and obtain their permission for the use of copyright material. The author apologizes for any errors or omissions and would be grateful if notified of any corrections that should be incorporated into future editions of the book.

The following permissions have been obtained:

Photos, taken by Wilber Bowe, Frank Farrell, Royce Vick, Robert Matulac, Steve Vincent, Steve Streeter, Leon Toyne, and the map structure from The Ground You Stand Upon, by Joshua Bowe and Wilber Bowe.

Material from Dr. Stuart Poticha's Tropics Lightning Flashed newsletter, material from Robert Kunkel's book Walking Point, and material from Sarah Blum's article in the Wisconsin Highground newsletter.

Articles and photos and After-Action Reports from Air Cavalry Division website. The United States Army does not claim copyright on any material but requests that proper credit be attributed to all Army photos and documents.

To ask permission to use any part of this work, email the publisher at brownmule7nam@gmail.com

To obtain a printed version of this book:

Amazon link: https://www.amazon.com/Books-Search/

To submit any additional information or corrections, email the author at:

brownmule7nam@gmail.com

Thank You for taking the time to read our story. Reviews are most appreciated; please leave your review on Amazon.

Acknowledgment

I'd like to recognize all the kind individuals who helped contribute to the writing of this book. Their input, comments, and guidance helped tremendously in making this effort a success. Not only family and friends but many others are learning about the experiences of my brother and four of his closest buddies in Vietnam. The most heartwarming part of this endeavor is seeing the families of Vietnam veterans touched by this story. If you enjoyed reading this book or learned something from it, please let me know by posting on Amazon. It means a lot to their families and me. I would like to sincerely thank the following individuals who helped contribute to this book.

Amie Toyne and Casey Toyne

My brother's widow as she allowed me to use Leon's letters to create the book. She was so supportive throughout the process ad provided great input and feedback. Additionally, her youngest son Casey provided great feedback for the book.

Victor and Florence Toyne

The grandparents on my Dad's side were responsible for generating great content in the letters by asking Leon great questions during their numerous letters. They wrote letters and sent packages to Leon weekly and kept his morale high.

Joshua Bowe and Wilbur Bowe, authors of the outstanding book "The Ground You Stand Upon."

I cannot thank Josh Bowe and his Dad, Wilbur Bowe, enough. Their outstanding book is the driving force, which gave me the inspiration to tell my brother Leon's own story. Their book, which mirrors a lot of the operations and locations of my brother, helped me fill in many of the gaps, and accurately document his Vietnam tour.

Additionally, Josh helped me tremendously with the process of formatting the book, structure, and content, and how to ensure all copyright laws were addressed, etc.

Frank and Doug Farrell

Doug Farrell, the son of Frank Farrell and his dad Frank, I can't thank him enough. Doug, with the help of his Dad Frank, really helped fill gaps in the letters and provided great pictures of my brother and Frank Farrell.

Frank was a buddy who served with Leon in Vietnam and was mentioned several times in the letters. Additionally, he provided stories that supported the letters.

Steve Vincent's Family Members, Gene, and Loa Dawn Vincent

Gene Vincent and his wife, Loa Dawn, were very helpful, providing pictures and stories about Gene's brother Steve Vincent, who was a Combat Medic in Vietnam. Steve was a buddy of Leon's and was mentioned several times in Leon's letters. They also traveled together to Iowa while on leave.

Steve Streeter and Wife Gig

Steve Streeter and his wife Gig were very helpful. Steve provided great stories of his time in Vietnam.

Steve was a buddy of Leon's and was mentioned in Leon's letters. They also traveled together in Iowa. Additionally, Leon kept track of Steve and visited him after the Vietnam war.

Jerry Nicholson's sister Dorothy Frazier

Jerry Nicholson's sister Dorothy Frazier has allowed the use of Jerry's name and tell his stories. She helped fill additional gaps in the letters. Jerry was a buddy who was with Leon in Vietnam and Fort Leonardwood and wireman training. He served with Leon in Vietnam and was mentioned several times in the letters. Dorothy provided stories that supported the letters.

Toyne Family Members

My wife, Donna, supported me through the highs and lows of developing this book. She helped me edit and proofread the book. Additionally, my brother Steve, who provided input, and my daughter Jessica and son Jake who helped edit and proofread the book.

Dedication

I would like to dedicate this book, with the Vietnam letters, not discovered until 52 years later, in memory of my brother Leon Toyne, who passed away in 2018. Much too soon, and most likely contributed by his serving in the jungles of Vietnam. He courageously served in the Army from 1965-1967, with 10 1/2 months in Vietnam under incredible circumstances, until he was injured. Although Leon was a non-volunteer draftee into the Army at the age of 21, you'll see in the letters he honorably served and was dedicated to doing the best job he could with the hand he was dealt. In these letters, he never once talked badly about his country, just about the KP (kitchen police) mess sergeant, which he hated because he despised KP duty. He kept upbeat and deflected the conversation from his dangerous daily routine, being more concerned about people back home and talking about them in his unique flowery language.

These letters were written to my Grandma Florence & Grandpa Vic, mom Freda, dad Merritt, sister Connie, brother Steve, and myself. Special recognition should be given to Grandma Florence and Grandpa Vic, who wrote him 100s of letters on a fixed income and sent him weekly care packages of tobacco, cigars, Kool-Aid, gum, newspapers, funny papers, candy, etc. The majority of letters were written to my grandparents, in which he tempered how bad things were and how he didn't know from day to day if he would make it through his 12 months in Vietnam. I know my grandparents contributed to his safe return by keeping him upbeat and helping him maintain a positive attitude. He didn't directly come out and say it, but you could read between the lines. Even to the extent he commented, he didn't want to write directly to my brother and me until the dangerous part of his tour was over so as not to draw attention to him in Vietnam, by getting our hopes up in case things went bad.

I would also like to dedicate this book to Frank Farrell, Steve Vincent, Steve Streeter, and Jerry Nicholson and their families and friends. These individuals were like brothers to Leon, and as indicated in his letters, they developed a bond that helped them cope with the daily dangers of their tour in Vietnam. I have no doubt this bond helped them survive the ordeal and allowed them to return home to their families.

It's tough to imagine what individuals like my brother and his 5th Bn/7th Cav brothers went through day-to-day in Vietnam, not knowing if they would make it back home in one piece. I know my 21 years of military service pales in comparison to individuals like these who served in Vietnam. We need to continue to recognize them and tell their stories.

By Mike Toyne

About the Author

Mike Toyne is retired and lives in Omaha, Nebraska, along with his wife, Donna. Mike is a 1974 graduate of Lohrville Community High School, Lohrville, Iowa. He initially enlisted in the Air Force in 1974. After serving four years in the Air Force, he separated from the Air Force to use his education benefits. He attended college at Montana State University, graduating in 1986 graduating with a master's degree in Education, with Exercise Psychology, and teaching and coaching emphasis. He also received an ROTC commission and re-entered the Air Force in 1986. He's a retired Air Force officer and government civilian, having worked 40 years in military operations, which included planning support for the nation's nuclear strategic deterrence mission. Mike enjoys running and biking, having finished several ½ and full marathons and ridden RAGBRAI across Iowa. In 2023, he published Brown Mule 7. A true story of his brother's Vietnam War experience.

Mike Toyne

Leon Toyne's 1966-67 Vietnam letters were the inspiration for this book. He passed away in 2018 at the age of 73. His contributions were written over fifty years ago in the jungles of Vietnam, as letters home to his grandparents and parents. He is survived by his wife Amie and children Cody, Lanette, Casey, and several grandchildren. Known as a dedicated and hard worker, he worked on local ranches in the area while he attended Lander Valley High School, graduating in 1964.

After graduation, Leon was drafted into the U.S. Army on October 26, 1965, and served during the Vietnam War. He received several decorations for his actions in Vietnam and was wounded at the end of his tour, spending several months in hospitals overseas before being transferred to Fitzsimmons Hospital in Denver, CO.

Once out of the service, he worked on ranches in the Lander area. In 1968 at a 4th of July rodeo in Lander, Wyoming, he met the love of his life for 49 years, Amie Annis. On April 5, 1969, they were married in Casper, WY. Shortly after their wedding, in 1969, they moved to Iowa to work with his uncle Daryl on the family farm and hog operation. In 1979 they moved back to Wyoming, buying a cattle ranch and making their home on Gooseberry Creek near Worland, WY. In 1979, he began work at the Worland Sugar Factory, balancing factory work and ranching. In 2006 they moved to Otto, WY. He retired from the factory after 28 years in 2008. They lived in Otto until 2011 when the ranch was sold. Finally, in 2012, Leon and Amie bought their last farm in the Pavillion, WY, area.

Leon and his faithful cow horse, Jake

Leon and his wife Amie on Leon's style of vacation, a 28-mile pack trip to go fishing at Yellowstone Meadows by the Yellowstone River

Table of Contents

About the Author 11

    Army Combat Infantry Badge – Military Operational Specialty 15

    7th Cavalry Returns at Fort Carson, Colorado 19

    PREFACE 22

    Chapter 1: I'm Going, No Turning Back - USNS Gaffey Final Voyage 25

    Chapter 2: Attack on An Khe - Guarding Highway 19 35

    Chapter 3: Building Bunkers to Protect from Mortars 45

    Chapter 4: Phu Cat – Friendly Villagers 51

    Chapter 5: Papa San 58

    Chapter 6: Doc Vincent and Bravo Company 71

    Chapter 7: Christmas in Vietnam 83

    Chapter 8: On the Green-Line - In A Company 88

    Chapter 9: Scout Dogs Save Lives 94

    Chapter 10: LZ English – LZ Hump 105

    Chapter 11: LZ Pony - LZ Sandra 116

    Chapter 12: Steve Streeter and 12th Evac Hospital at Cu Chi 124

    Chapter 13: Brown Mule 7 134

    Chapter 14: Guarding the Dump 138

    Chapter 15: Transferring from 5th Bn/7th Cav - Building Barracks 142

    Chapter 16: Injured – A Long Road to Recovery 151

    Chapter 17: The Non-Welcome Home – The Enemy Within 160

    Bibliography 169

    Glossary 172

Army Combat Infantry Badge – Military Operational Specialty

Army Combat Field Wireman: SP4 Leon Toyne was a field wireman during his tour in Vietnam. Typical duties of this Military Operational Specialty (MOS) include the installation of telephones and switchboards, and the laying wire and cable. Tactical Switching Operators and Field Wiremen adjust equipment for proper operation. They recover wire, locate wire system faults, and operate switchboards. He performed his duties as a wireman in Vietnam base camps, landing zones, and in the jungles of various parts of the Central Highlands of Vietnam. It required him to venture out of camps and LZs at night to repair radio communication wires in the jungle without the use of light to avoid Vietcong detection. Communication lines were vital for leadership critical operations decision-making.

SP4 Toyne was awarded the United States Army Combat Infantry Badge for being personally present and under hostile fire while in a unit actively engaged in ground combat with the enemy during his tour in Vietnam from 1966-1967. In addition, he was awarded the National Defense Medal, Vietnam Service Medal, and the Vietnam Campaign Medal.

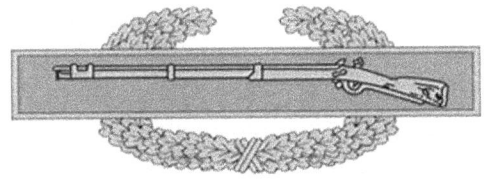

United States Army Combat Infantry Badge

The Combat Infantry Badge (CIB) is awarded to Army enlisted infantry, infantry, or special forces officers in the grade of Colonel or below, as well as warrant officers with infantry or special forces MOS.

The recipient must be personally present and under hostile fire while in a unit actively engaged in ground combat with the enemy. Awards will not be presented to general officers or members of headquarters companies of units larger in size than the brigade.

The CIB and the Expert Infantry Badge were created primarily as a means of recognizing the sacrifices of the infantrymen who were disproportionately likely to be killed or wounded during World War II.

"Everyone should care what the infantrymen who wear it risked breaking their mothers' hearts."

"They went to war and knocked on death's door." Unknown

"War never leaves you—it is like grief…you get used to it. It is a scar hidden by clothing; you wear forever. People don't see it, but you know it is there." Unknown

Emblems Taken from the National Archives, College Park, Maryland

Four additional contributions to this book are from Frank Farrell, Steve Vincent, Steve Streeter, Jerry Nicholson, and their families. Four key individuals my brother spoke fondly of in his letters. They served with Leon Toyne from training in Ft Carson, Colorado, through serving in Vietnam from August 1966 – July 1967. Their duties as Radio Telephone Operator, Combat Medic, War Zone Dental Medic, and Field Wireman are described below and mentioned throughout the book. These are three HHQ company critical support functions vital to the successful operation of combat units in Vietnam.

Army Radio Telephone Operator (RTO): SP4 Frank Farrell, as an RTO, was responsible for reporting conflicts or firefights to headquarters, which would, in turn, provide support, whether air or ground, to units that were in conflict. The radio operator goes where the commander goes. So, where you would see the company commander, you see the RTO right behind him. The enemy targets the RTO because they know the commander of the company/squad is nearby. For this reason, the RTO's life expectancy in Vietnam was short.

Frank Farrell was awarded the Combat Infantry Badge for being personally present and under hostile fire while in a unit actively engaged in ground combat with the enemy during his tour in Vietnam from 1966-1967. Additionally, he was awarded the National Defense Medal, Vietnam Service Medal, and the Vietnam Campaign Medal.

Army Combat Medic: SP4 Steve Vincent was a combat medic during his tour in Vietnam. The combat medic is a unique type of soldier. They put themselves in the middle of life-threatening battles, but they do so in love, not take lives. Not only must they work with limited resources to save lives, but they must also do so under intense pressure, knowing that their own lives could come to an end at any moment. While other soldiers are trying to avoid enemy fire and head for cover, the Medic would be seen coming to the aid of a fellow soldier while under fire.

Steve Vincent was awarded the Bronze Star. The Bronze Star is a United States decoration awarded to members of the United States Armed Forces for either heroic achievement, heroic service, meritorious achievement, or meritorious service in a combat zone. In Steve's case, he was awarded it for valor and heroic effort as a Combat Medic in Vietnam from 1966-1967. Additionally, he was awarded the National Defense Medal, Vietnam Service Medal, and the Vietnam Campaign Medal.

Army War Zone Dental Medic: SP4 Steve Streeter was a 12th Evac Hospital medic during his tour in Vietnam. The War Zone Dental Medic is in a unique position in a war zone environment. Not only must they work with limited resources and a tough environment to put soldiers' faces, jaws, and mouths back together, but they hope to lead a normal life after war-induced injury.

Steve Streeter was awarded the National Defense Medal, Vietnam Service Medal, and the Vietnam Campaign Medal for his tour in Vietnam from 1966-1967.

Army Combat Field Wireman: SP4 Jerry Nicholson was a field wireman, and their typical duties included the installation of telephones and switchboards and laying wire and cable. Tactical Switching Operators and Field Wiremen adjust equipment for proper operation. They recover wire, locate wire system faults, and operate switchboards. He performed his duties as a wireman in Vietnam base camps, landing zones, and various parts of the Central Highlands of Vietnam.

Jerry Nicholson was awarded the Combat Infantry Badge for being personally present and under hostile fire while in a unit actively engaged in ground combat with the enemy during his tour in Vietnam from 1966-1967. Additionally, he was awarded the National Defense Medal, Vietnam Service Medal, and the Vietnam Campaign Medal.

7th Cavalry Returns at Fort Carson, Colorado

Fort Carson's new 5th Battalion, 7th Cavalry, first commanded by George Armstrong Custer 100 years ago, boasts a heritage of four Distinguished Unit Citations, two Korean Presidential Unit Citations, a Philippine Presidential Unit Citation, and the Chryssoun Aristion Andries, Greece's Gold Medal for Bravery. The 7th Cavalry was at the Battle of Little Bighorn in Montana on June 25th, 1876, when Custer's five troops of 264 cavalrymen faced more than 6,000 Sioux, Cheyenne, and Apache Indians. The result was history, and 14 troopers were awarded the Medal of Honor. The 5th Battalion 7th Cavalry comes to life again at Fort Carson, not too far from where it was given the mission of guarding the western frontier in the days of Indian warfare.

The 7th Cavalry Regiment was constituted on July 28, 1866, at Fort Riley, Kansas. Its motto, the Seventh First, signifies the regiment and its successors came first in the action of its members. The 7th Cavalry's regimental crest, horseshoe-shaped with four nails on the right and three on the left, boasts an arm and a saber used in the Indian campaigns. The blue and gold colors reflect the old Cavalry. Across the top is "Garry Owen." The regimental name Garry Owen, Gaelic for Owen's Garden, comes from the 5th Royal Irish Lancers, who frequented Garry Owen, a suburb of Limerick, Ireland. A tavern took the now-famous name, and a song was born. Later, across the seas, General Custer approved the name and the song so popular among tough Irish immigrants and Civil War veterans in the 7th Cavalry.

They faced such famous Indian chiefs as Crazy Horse, Sitting Bull, and Joseph of the Sioux. Indian campaigns were against the Comanche from 1868 to 1875, in Montana in 1873, in Dakota in 1874, at Little Big Horn from 1876-77, against Nez Perce in 1877, and in Pine Ridge 1890-91. Troops C, E, F, I, and L were annihilated at Little Big Horn, where Custer made his famous last stand. Later they were in pursuit of Pancho Villa on the Mexican border. The regimental colors were flown in the Philippine Islands as far back as 1878. During World War II, the 7th Cavalry won a Distinguished Unit Citation in Luzon as well as the Philippine Presidential Unit Citation. The 1st Cavalry Division made the initial entry into Japan, and the 7th Cavalry had the honor of escorting General Douglas MacArthur into Tokyo. Twenty-eight days after the Korean fighting started, the 7th Cavalry Regiment was at Pohang-Dong for the first of nine campaigns. *(Taken from the May 6th, 1966 issue of Fort Carson's newspaper, The Mountaineer)*

In Vietnam, the First Cavalry Division was a total concept of warfare identified as Air Mobile. The new fighting concept battlefield was a nightmare for the enemy. The Air Cavalry would drop in front of, behind, or even right in the middle of the opposition and overwhelm enemy soldiers. The concept befuddled enemy soldiers and even confused their commanders. The North Vietnamese were perplexed by the swiftness of the 1st Cavalry aerial onslaught and that the 1st Cavalry was always on the offensive.

The 1st Cavalry Division was the only division to serve in Vietnam and win a Presidential Unit Citation. During the 82 months of continuous combat operations in Vietnam, there were 25 Medals of Honor, 120 Distinguished Service Crosses, 2700 Silver Stars, and many Purple Hearts awarded to the 1st Cavalry Division. The 1st Cavalry has 5,410 names engraved on The Wall in Washington D.C. Each name represents those who gave all, not returning home. It's a sad fact, but the 1st Cavalry had more soldiers killed in action in the Vietnam War than any unit. *(From Vietnam National Archives, College Station, Maryland)*

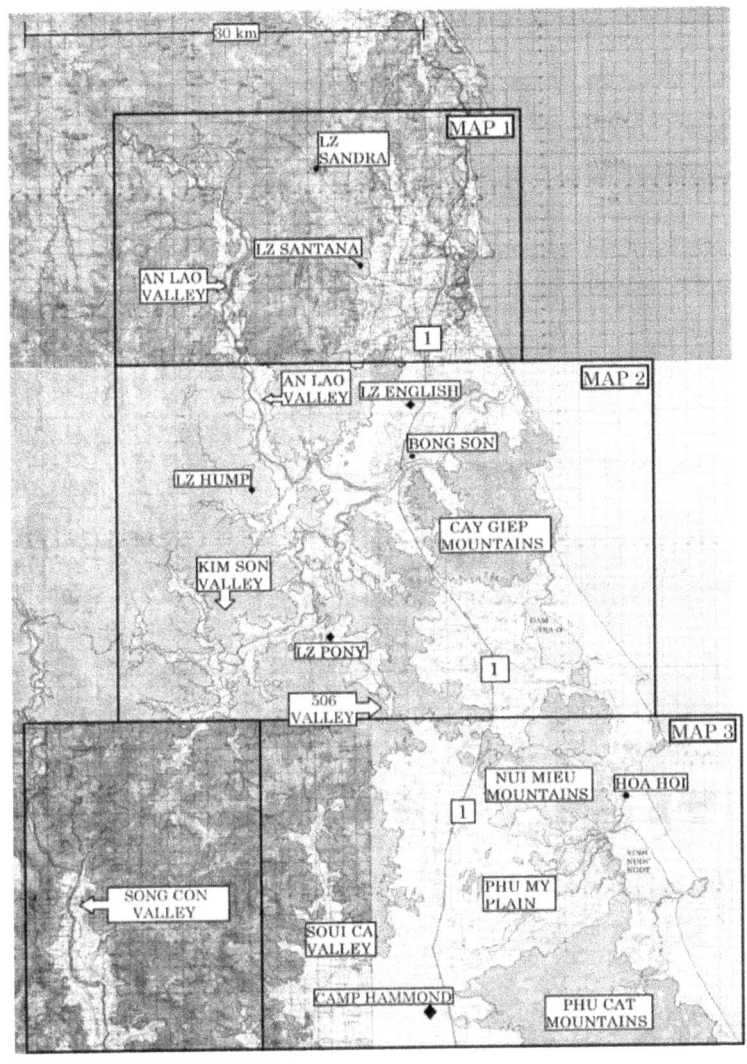

Bases and LZ for the 5th Battalion, 7th Cavalry
Operated in Vietnam from 1966-1967

Taken from the National Archives, College Park,
Maryland

PREFACE

In February 2018, my brother passed away at the age of 73 from a blood disorder, which doctors said more than likely was contributed by his serving in the jungles of Vietnam around chemicals, namely Agent Orange. Later in 2018, Leon's widow Amie, asked me if I'd like to read the 85+ Vietnam letters Leon wrote home from 1966-1967. This is what started my quest after discovering 52-year-old letters written home from Vietnam. They were from August 1966 - July 1967, and were about where he lived and fought in the Central Highlands and Coastal Plains of Vietnam, with the 5th Battalion, 7th Cavalry's mission of "search and destroy" the North Vietnamese Army and Vietcong enemy.

Leon was drafted into the Army to serve in Vietnam when I was 11 years old. All I remember was the news on TV was bad, and my parents and grandparents were really worried about him. Until I read the letters, I had no idea what he went through over there. However, I recall when he came home, he never wanted to talk about it, even though I asked. He also was jittery around loud noises, and you didn't want to startle him by walking up from behind, unannounced.

Reading his letters brought tears to my eyes. They were written to my grandparents, but it was as if he was talking to me. Since they were written to my grandparents, he softened some of the language, but he still talked about how bad it was in Vietnam and how they were losing guys, etc. He described his duties of going into the jungle outside the Green-Line to repair Commo lines at night, without light, for fear the enemy would see him and take him out. There were so many questions that I wanted to ask him but couldn't. The letters were very detailed, so I decided I would accomplish further research based on the letters and try to fill in the gaps to try to answer my questions. I realized this was a story that needed to be expanded on and properly told to his family and friends. They need to know what he went through in Vietnam and how it shaped his life, making him a changed person when he returned home. But how do you write a story about something that happened over 50 years ago without the main character around to help you?

Initially, I started out interpreting my brother's handwritten letters and typing them up for his widow Amie and her family so they could know what he went through. He was a hero who was never properly recognized for his Vietnam service, like other Vietnam veterans when they returned home. Additionally, how did this Vietnam experience and serious head injury impact his life? My brother was injured in Vietnam by being struck in the forehead with rock debris from an explosion while clearing an area for construction. The blast left him with a hole in his head the size of a baseball, and it's a miracle he survived. He had brain surgery which totaled eight operations, that included putting a plate in his head. Through all of this, including some symptoms of PTSD, he stayed the course and didn't place blame. He persevered and became a successful cattle rancher in Wyoming, and through meeting his loving and supporting wife Amie, was able to raise three great kids who learned the value of dedication and hard work to achieve success.

I was very fortunate to come across in my research "The Ground You Stand Upon," an outstanding book written by Joshua Bowe with his father, Wilbur Bowe. Joshua Bowe has been so helpful, giving me the support, knowledge, and inspiration to expand on my brothers' letters. Their book is about the 5th Battalion, 7th Cavalry A Company in Vietnam Aug 1966 – August 1967, which took place during the same timeframe and the majority of the locations and operations where my brother was while in the 5th Battalion, 7th Cavalry Higher Headquarters Company. Additionally, my brother filled in A Company for a short while when they were shorthanded.

After researching the letters and talking to other veterans, I realized this story, like many other Vietnam veterans, needed to be shared with a larger audience. In my research of my brothers' letters, I was able to find four families who wanted to recognize their loved ones who served in Vietnam with my brother by telling their stories in the book.

My intent in this book is to reference some of the information from "The Ground You Stand Upon," where there are similarities and expand on some distinct differences. "Brown Mule 7" addresses the Vietnam experience from a different perspective by looking through the eyes of two Combat Field Wireman, a Radio Operator, a Combat Medic, and a War Zone Dental Medic. Additional contributions are from Frank Farrell and his son Doug. Frank served with my brother as a Radio Operator (RTO) in the HHQ Company. Also, Gene Vincent and his wife, Loa Dawn, provided contributions for Gene's brother Steve Vincent, who served and traveled with my brother while serving as a Combat Medic in Bravo Company. Additionally, there are contributions from Steve Streeter and his wife, Gig. Steve was a 12th Evac Hospital medic and a good friend of my brother in Iowa. They traveled together and stayed in touch after Vietnam. Finally, Jerry Nicholson's sister Dorothy. Jerry served with my brother as a Field Wireman in the HHQ Company. These individuals performed critical duties, which were vital to ensuring mission operational success, by providing critical communications and medical care for the 5th Battalion, 7th Cavalry soldiers.

Through this book, I intend to honestly and properly represent those Vietnam veterans and others who honorably served and educate others on the sacrifices these individuals and their families went through. The recognition for the Vietnam veteran was too little too late, and it hurt their adjustment back to civilian life.

Chapter 1: I'm Going, No Turning Back - USNS Gaffey Final Voyage

29 Jul 66

Dear Grandma & Grandpa,

I just received your letter, and I got a little spare time, so will try and answer it. The plane ride didn't make me sick at all. We only had to wait 15 minutes for the plane. It traveled 300 miles an hour. We got to Denver at 7:30 our time. Then the next plane left from Denver at 8:30, but we got bumped off. The next plane left at 11:30, so I got in Colorado Springs at 1:00, took a taxi, and got back to Fort Carson, signing in at 1:30 PM. We didn't have to be in until noon, so I wasn't AWOL. On the first day, we had about 80 AWOL, and now they cut it down to about 20. There is one from my platoon that went AWOL. One of my buddies from Wyoming, he's from Laramie.

The first night I got here I was sure homesick, but I soon got over it. My new address is PFC Leon E. Toyne, US55808833 HHC 5th BN, 7th CAV APO San Francisco, CA. We've been buying up supplies to last us three months. They said it would be that long before we see a Post Exchange (PX). They've been inspecting our gear for readiness.

Well, I got the word, there's no getting out of it, I'm going for sure now. I'll be in California by the time you receive this letter. We'll get there by plane and will only wait 15 minutes before we board the ship.

Well, there's not much I can say now, just kind of waiting for the big move. It's been raining quite a bit out here. The temperature has been 70 to 80 degrees, or near as bad as Iowa. Well, I will close for now. I have run out of things to say. Be sure and put this APO on my letters, or I'll never get them.

Leon

2 Aug 66

Dear Grandma & Grandpa,

Well, I'm on the ship now. The name of it is the USNS Gaffey. It's big, they will be hauling 2400 of us. Some of the troops are coming from other Forts. I've been here two days now. We are moving out at 2:00 this afternoon. They have so many troops that they had to make more room for bunks. This sure is an old-looking ship.

Another ship just came in this morning. It is called the Patricia and it came from Hawaii. There must have been some kind of dog show because they had about 50 or more dogs.

I don't think too much of California. They say it's sunny, but all I see are clouds and smog. I am about 17 miles from San Francisco. I can see the Golden Gate Bridge from my dock, and we'll pass under it before long. I left Fort Carson at 2:00 this morning, Monday morning, and landed at Travis airport, at about 4:00. Then we went by bus to the dock.

Well, I will try and finish this letter. We are on our way now. This ship sure is rocking, and I'm getting a little light-headed, but it's not too bad so far. I sure hated to leave the states. It just didn't seem possible that I'm on my way.

We passed by Alcatraz, now I know why not many ever escaped. Then we went under the Golden Gate Bridge. Well, we are well on our way now. We sure had a lot of guys get sick. It doesn't seem to bother me too much. I didn't feel too good at first, but I'm getting over it. When it storms or the water gets rough, I get pretty dizzy, but otherwise, I'm able to navigate.

I'm on laundry detail, not too bad of a job. I go to work at 8:00 and get off at 3:00 in the afternoon. All I do is separate the towels, jackets, sheets, etc. It's all the ship's laundry. And another good thing is we don't have to wait in line for chow. The head of the laundry department just takes us to the front of the line. The chow isn't too good, but I guess it's better than nothing.

How's the weather back there now? Is it as hot as it was when I was there? It's pretty cool here for a change. It will probably be 30 days before you get this letter because it will be sent from Okinawa. We aren't going to get to stop at Hawaii.

It sure is easy to get lost on this ship. I was just getting to where I could find the mess hall, and then they moved us again to another *compartment. I know one thing for sure. I never want to be a sailor, because I like the land too well. This ship we are on is run by civilians. It's too old and dirty to be a Navy ship.*

Well, I better cut this off for now. I sent my right address to Mom, so you can use that one until I send another.

Love, Leon

August 2nd, 1966 - Soldiers of the 5/7th Cav wait to board the USNS Gaffey

USNS Gaffey, photo by Martin Bierschach

From The Ground You Stand Upon, written by Joshua and Wilber Bowe

The 5th Battalion, 7th Cavalry (5/7th Cav), was one of nine infantry battalions that belonged to the 1st Air Cavalry Division, responsible for ridding the Central Highlands and Eastern Coastal Plains of communist forces. The other battalions, which included the 1st and 2nd Battalions, and 7th Cavalry, had already been in Vietnam for just over a year. With the massive military buildup that would occur between 1965 and 1967, the 5/7th Cav was formed as a brand-new battalion on April 6. They trained at Fort Carson, Colorado, and the Battalion departed on its historic maiden voyage from a foggy San Francisco Bay on August 2nd, spending 18 days at sea and enduring a typhoon in the South

China Sea before arriving at the Port of Qui Nhon on August 20th, 1966.

They were transported inland, into the heart of the Central Highlands, to Camp Radcliff, the 1st Air Cavalry's base camp, more commonly referred to as An Khe (a nearby city). They would spend approximately two weeks building their new battalion area and undergoing additional training in preparation for their first mission.

21 Aug 66

Dear Grandma & Grandpa,

Well, I'm in Vietnam now. I got off the ship on the 19th, a barge picked us and our gear up. They took us ashore and they had a big brass band, with everyone playing for us. Then we were loaded on buses and they hauled us to a cargo plane. We unloaded everything and put it on the plane. I guess I have gotten over being air sick on planes because that sure was a rough-riding plane. There were 152 of us stacked in there, and we had to stand up. We were only in the air for 15 minutes. We landed, then buses picked us up and hauled us to our location. There is nothing here, as we had to build everything.

We slept on cots with nets over us in big tents. It's just like camping, you might say. We wash and shave in our steel pots and draw our water from a water wagon.

This area is mountains, and trees, and down where we are camped is swamp grass. We are in a pretty safe area. We got till the first of October to get our camp set up before the monsoon season hits. That's where it rains 24 hours a day. So, we shouldn't be in too much contact with the enemy till after then.

In camp, we don't have to pack our gear and rifle around all the time. They give us each 300 rounds of ammunition, so it's pretty heavy to pack all that around.

We are close to a town called An Khe, which is supposed to carry the supplies we need. There are all kinds of equipment over here, building roads, and things. It's kind of like a little village going up, but it sure is lonesome.

We have to get all our money changed to the script, and it looks just like play money over here, so I decided it's a good time to pay you that $40.00 I owe you. Borrowed it when Bill T. and I were back there that time. I hadn't forgotten it. It might take me a while, but I always pay my bills.

I got the letter you sent after I got here, it sure was a welcome piece of news. That's the only thing I look forward to around here, are letters from home.

What happened to Dad? Brother Steve wrote me and said he hurt his neck again. That kind of work is just too hard for him. He better quit, that's how I think I got that hernia from lifting too much. I sure pray he's all right, it sure worries me, him working that hard like that.

I suppose school is starting pretty soon. Sometimes I wish I was back in school again. You just don't realize how good you had it until you're in a place like this.

When we stopped in Okinawa, they let us get off for about 8 hours. Me and my buddies went to one of these air-conditioned restaurants and stuffed ourselves with good food. You could buy big cheeseburgers for 15 cents and all their food was cheap. It was good too, after eating that stuff on the ship. The military part of Okinawa is modern, but the rest is old-fashioned. Horse-drawn carts with weaved baskets in them. People wash clothes just like you see in the history books, villages, etc. You can guess how hot it is here, so hot that the envelopes stick together, so I have to tape them.

Well, I guess I run out of things to say, so will close for now.

Love, Leon

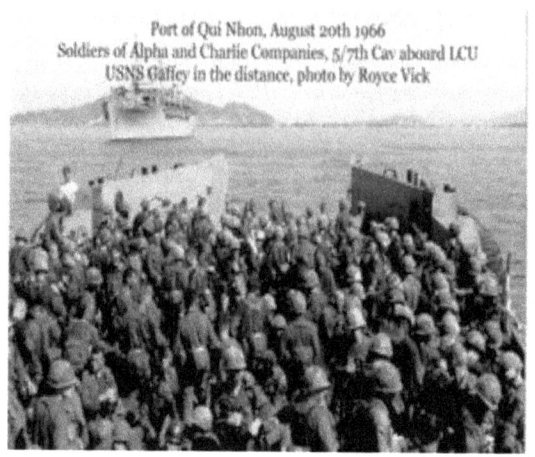

20 August 1966, 5th/7th Cav arrive at Qui Nhon, photo by Royce Vick

7 Aug 66

Dear Grandma & Grandpa,

I was so happy when I received your letters. I am glad everything is alight. I got the pictures all right, and they were in good shape when I received them.

Grandma, you talk of guard duty I do. We start at 7:00 at night, and we walk for two hours on, and two hours off. A person can be pretty alert when the hours aren't too long at a time.

Well, Grandpa, you should be able to keep pretty up to date on the games & sports now that you don't have to work. Say that trip you talked about Warren & Ella Mae and Shirley & Colleen went on. I got a buddy in my platoon that lives up there near Duluth, near the Canadian border, isn't it?

Don't be surprised if you don't hear from me for a while, we got to go on a mission that is supposed to last 45 days, so it might be a while before I can write again. It's so darn hot here the only time I can write is in the morning or evening because my hand sweats so bad it blots the paper. I tape all of my envelopes because they stick together so bad.

You ask about Steve Vincent; I see him every day. He's like me, he isn't enjoying it a bit, but he's getting along ok. You talk about salt pills. They give us all we want, plus other pills for malaria and other diseases. That's one thing, they don't want us to get sick.

It's been raining a little bit every day, so that keeps us cool. The other day I drew KP. They keep you pretty busy on that. I started at 4:00 in the morning, and got done at 8:30 that night; so I put in a long day.

I go down to the Enlisted Men Club, it's called. Every company built one after a while. They have cold pop, potato chips, and things like that. It's just a place to relax.

I got your other letter, just as I was writing this one, so the mail is coming through really well., I just finished eating, so will try and finish this letter.

I am starting to gain back some weight, so I guess food is pretty good. We eat on picnic tables now. We are starting to get things looking like somebody lives here now. We've been making foot lockers out of ammo boxes to put our gear and things in.

This unit joined the 1st Cav. We are Air Mobile. They are sending the whole 5th Division over here now, all of Fort Carson. They won't all be right in this area but will be in Vietnam somewhere.

They're giving us passes to go to town now. I haven't gone yet, but they say it is just like Okinawa.

Love, Leon

3 Sep 66

Dear Grandma & Grandpa,

I received your package on the 2nd. It sure was a welcome sight. It will come in really handy because we are going out on a mission Sunday. We will be out anywhere from 30 to 130 days. It depends on how much we get done there. Otherwise, we'd be doing the same old thing around here.

It's been raining here more than usual, so, therefore, it's not as hot when it rains.

I got a letter from Connie; she's beginning to realize she has a hard ole road to hoe. She wants to come home for Xmas, but she hasn't decided whether she should or not. She claims ole "you know who" is over in Turkey, and that he will be in Vietnam soon. I sure hope he has to spend a year over here. This kind of life will straighten anyone out.

We sure are having a hard time laying cement. Looks like it will be a year before we get it done, and then it will be time to rotate, but I don't care. Let somebody else have the place. It rains so much now it just ruins any cement that we get down. Right now, I just have a cardboard floor under my cot. It is just about the next thing to nothing, but it does help a little.

They just issued me more fatigues, and now I have four pairs of boots to wear out. I guess that should last me 11 more months. This climate here sure is hard on equipment, and we have to keep things well-oiled, or they will rust right in your hand practically.

The way I got it figured, is we will go on only 3-4 missions at the most, but some of these missions will last 3 months. Now they stay out till they get it done, or send more troops to help finish it.

Well, I haven't got any more to say, other than I'm going on my first mission, so I will have a lot of interesting things to tell you in my next letter. I will close till next time.

Leon

P.S., Thank you millions for the box of goodies.

Moment of Truth is Near for 1ˢᵗ Cavalry's Newest Battalion (Columbus Enquirer, Columbus, Ga., Friday, September 9, 1966)

AN KHE, Vietnam (UPI) – The moment of truth is fast approaching for the 1ˢᵗ Air Cavalry Division's newest Battalion – the moment when men will face death in the jungle hell battlefield of Vietnam.

Some of the men are worried. Maybe pint-sized PFC Timothy Payne is too, but he doesn't show it. "Man, those Vecee can't kill me; I owe too much money. I'm paying alimony." Payne is from Galien, Mich. He is a little guy. And he has his troubles because of it. Like this afternoon when he and his buddies were standing in line to get an issue of jungle boots. "Man, they just have to have my size 4 1/2," he said. The quartermaster did, and he and his companions laced up their new boots.

Black Mud Everywhere

The thick black mud is everywhere this time of year in the Central Highlands, home to the new unit; 5th Battalion, 7th Cavalry is hacking out of the jungle for itself. So far, the men of the Battalion have not faced the enemy. They arrived in Vietnam on Aug. 20 to bring the brigade up to strength. But they know that any day now, they will trudge out into the jungle hunting communists to kill.

They know too that some of them aren't coming back. Like some of the guys, they've replaced. "But they're more than willing," says Sgt. Major Robert Meyer, a giant of a man from Newport, Ky. "Morale is especially high, were ready."

Been in Training

Since the Battalion was formed, the men have had extensive physical training. They believe they are in good fighting condition. Lt Col Trevor (Ted) Swett of Columbus, Ga., battalion commander, could not be prouder of his men and their intensive training program. "Even the 18 days on a ship coming over has not taken the edge off." He said, "Could you believe 85 laps around the deck of the ship is three miles." Besides the running and physical training aboard the ship, the men fired their M-16s off the fantail and attended lectures to learn more about the war they would soon be fighting, the enemy they were out to kill, and who was out to kill them.

Some Will be Hurt

"There are advantages to coming to war as a unit," Swett said. "One of them is that you know all of the men personally. There's one problem, though. "Some of them are going to get hurt." As he said this, the battalion commander's grin disappeared for a split second. Then it reappeared, and he added: "But we feel we are big enough to take it in stride." The Colonel said he could not ask for better troops. "Three-fourths of his officers, he said, hold the Expert Infantry Badge, and more than half of them have Ranger training." "Fort Carson outdid itself to give me the cream of the crop," he said. "The ultimate result is my troops will stay alive."

Close to An Khe

The battalion base camp is located only a couple of miles from the once sleepy village of An Khe, which is now a GI honky tonk haven where soldiers can buy anything from beer to female companionship. But only a few of the men have seen An Khe. Passes are few. There is so much work to do putting the finishing touches on a modern military fighting machine and its home camp. For example, there's 1st Sgt Haskell Westmoreland of Beckley, W. Va. He's busy working night and day whipping Charlie Company into shape. "We're over here for just one thing," he said. "And that's kill Viet Cong."

Chapter 2: Attack on An Khe - Guarding Highway 19

7 Sep 66

Dear Grandma & Grandpa,

I received your most welcome letter today, so will let you know what's happening. I'm sitting on top of a big bald mountain, about 40 miles from An Khe. We just got a communication system set up here. It's so we can see the Viet Cong coming and can radio ahead. Then we will bring mortar fire in on them.

It rains and it's foggy up here all the time. I don't do much of anything outside of operating a radio once in and while. About 100 Viet Cong tried to take over An Khe last night, but they didn't get the job done. That's the town that's 2 miles from our Main Camp.

They have been transporting the mail by helicopter from the Main Camp up to the mountain I'm on, so will try and get this letter out from here. We are acting as kind of a guard to this Highway 19 that's where all the road supplies come in from. We see that the Viet Cong don't use this road to their advantage. I got Jocelyn's letter, so tell her that I'll write when I get back off this mission, it's hard to write up here, and get the mail out.

I'm still bunking with the same buddy I always did. We got a pup tent pitched right down in the draw, where we sleep on a hillside. Steve V. is set up right across from us on the other side of the hill in a bunker. Ole Noseep, my other buddy is with the line company, on the highway guarding it.

My tent leaks a little, but outside of that, the sleeping conditions are great. I get plenty of sleep. This is a pretty safe area. The outfit that was here before us were here for 35 days, and they had never seen anything.

I got a letter from Donna the other day, guess she's getting ready for school to start. Grandpa, how does Lake City's football team look by now? We get a newspaper once a week, but it doesn't talk much about sports. All you read is what's happening in Vietnam. They do manage to get the funny paper to us every Sunday anyway.

They feed us two hot meals a day, and a C-ration, so the food isn't too bad. It is flown in by helicopter too. The wind blows all the time, and you feel like you could touch the clouds, were so high. I sure am enjoying the Kool-Aid and Fizzies. They sure do hit the spot. All our water tastes like rubber after it sits in those rubber barrels for a long time.

Will close this up till next time. I got the pictures. Thank you. Leon

P.S. Tell Mom and Men I am all right in case they don't get a letter from me.

Comments from interviewing Frank "Hazel" Farrell: Frank said, "One of my jobs as an RTO was to post on this mountaintop at night, so I could look down in the valley and monitor for the enemy and call in air support, etc." He added, "The Comm suite we used to communicate with Battalion Leadership was on the back of a jeep, which was dropped in by a helicopter."

Hon Cong Mountain overlooking An Khe, source unknown

Courtesy of: Pat Costello from "The Valley of Crosses," reprinted from October 1971 "TYPHOON."

Near the border of Pleiku and Binh Dinh Provinces, the Dak Pihao Mountains tower above the surrounding hills and plains of the Central Highlands. Highway 19, beginning at the coastal port of Qui Nhon, winds its way westward to Pleiku through the highlands, passing through a narrow slit in these mountains known as the Mang Yang Pass.

Highway 19 is one lifeline that feeds the allied forces operating in the highlands at Pleiku, Kontum, and the border camps. For years the Communists have harassed traffic on Highway 19 and attempted to close it on numerous occasions. Once, over 17 years ago, they did. The graves of several hundred Frenchmen atop the northern rim of the Mang Yang Pass bear mute testimony to the Communist victory. They died within a few kilometers of their resting place. The story of their battle has been recorded for history in the fascinating work of the late French journalist Bernard B. Fall, The Street Without Joy (The Stackpole Company-1964).

12 Sep 66

Dear Grandma & Grandpa,

I received your letter today. I got a lot of time for a while, so decided I would write you a few lines now. My feet swelled up so bad they had to bring me off the mountain, but they are healing good now. So, I will be going back sometime this week. They swelled up due to being exposed to water for too long. It rains all day long, and it's foggy all day too. Your feet are wet 24 hours a day, and they can just take so much. Some of the other guys are having the same trouble.

Now, I just found out that I will have to be up there for at least three months. I never thought I would be cold in this country, but it's cold and wet on the mountain. Most of the time you're cold, then you sleep on the wet ground too. So, it isn't very pleasant up there.

Sometimes I think it's safer up there than it is in the Main Camp. The first night I got back they started shooting mortars at the Main Camp, but they didn't get away with it very long. About a dozen helicopters started swarming above them putting out 18,000 rounds a minute, so you know those Viet Cong didn't last long. That was each helicopter putting out that many rounds.

Up on the mountain, our outfit is firing mortars all night, so it's hard to get any sleep. Our tent is about 20 yards away from one of these mortars, so our tent shakes every time it fires. The first day we were up there, some of the guys put their tents too close to the helicopter pad. When the helicopters came in at about 150 mph, they bring a lot of wind with them, so anything that isn't tied down well, it blows away. I saw about 10 air mattresses go up in the air, and a few got in the chopper blades and there weren't much left but tiny pieces. At the same time, all the tents blew down, so it was a disaster area for a while.

That was an interesting article about the plowing match. I sure would like to see one of those contests sometime. Sounds like Iowa is getting more western all the time. All they need now is a beautiful country and some mountains.

Well, I don't know what's best; one place you're cold and wet all of the time, and then on the other, hot and sweaty. I think I like it better where it's hot. I think a person gets tired of being wet all the time.

Well, I am getting like you, and I just can't think of anything to say.

Today I helped the PLC clerk build a desk and chair for his work. He's the one who keeps us with the supplies we need. He orders more when we get low, and he's in charge of giving out supplies to the different companies.

There's a lot of paperwork involved in this job. Each item has to have about three or four copies before it can be used.

Well, now I have run out of things to say. So, until I fill you in on the action, so long till next time. This is the Toyne Press closing for the night.

Your tough but rugged Grandson is untouchable, unbelievable, undeniable, uncatchable & unable to get out of here for another 10 months and 18 days.

Best Wishes,

Leon E. Toyne

After Action Report (3 Sep 66 Attack on Camp Ratcliff, 17 September 1966, 1st Cavalry Division (Air Mobile) Headquarters, declassified 17 September 1978.

On the night of 3 September 1966, a VC platoon launched a mortar attack on Camp Radcliff. The base was hit by 119 mortar rounds over a 5-minute period, killing 4 soldiers and wounding 76, while 77 of the 1st Cavalry's 400-plus helicopters were damaged. The VCs were believed to have escaped. In early September, the PAVN/VC also attacked several ARVN military bases and ambushed an ARVN convoy. The attacks illustrated the fragility of the control of the area by the South Vietnamese government and the need to suppress the PAVN/VC forces.

20 Sep 66

Dear Grandma & Grandpa,

I received your letter a few days ago, so decided to write now while I have a little free time.

The weather up here on the mountain is great, not real hot and not too cold. It hasn't rained for three days now. I can't believe it. I think something is wrong. It's even started to dry up a little up here. Sounds like your prisoners get a little wild every once in and while, Grandma. We got guys that shoot themselves in the hand, and anything they can think of to go back to the states, but none of them try to commit suicide.

You ask about this mountain I'm on. It's about ½ mile across the top. There's a higher mountain than it, but not as bald. When we first got up here it was all green grass, but when the rain came, and with everyone driving all over it, now it's just a mud hole. There's an old cement building up here that has a hole at the top, and that's the only entrance to it. I cannot figure out what it could be. We throw our garbage in it and burn it. Sure is built solid, but not good for anything I can see. Maybe it belonged to some old Frenchman. I bet it has a lot of history behind it.

We were sleeping in little old pup tents, but now we got our bunker built. We have a lot of room for the three of us to sleep, even with our gear. Our communications station is a big old building made out of sandbags with steel rods supporting them.

Those clippings you sent were pretty interesting. I was hoping somebody would send what everybody was telling me, about going to the plowing match. I see they don't expect to have very high corn yields this year. If you got a ¼ of the rain we get, you would have corn to throw away.

This mountain we are on is 40 miles from An Khe, so we were a long way from the action. There are switchbacks up to this mountain we are on, so trucks can get up here. Our chow comes in by truck in the morning and helicopter at night.

We got some good blankets, and a sleeping bag, so we don't get cold when we can keep our gear dry. Well, ran out of things to say, so will close till next time.

Leon

24 Sep 66

Dear Grandma & Grandpa,

I received your most welcome letter at 8:00 this morning when I had just woken up. The sergeant delivered the mail to our hutch (bunker). All of a sudden, the other two guys in here with me started to look at each other, as there was a funny smell stinking our home. It was the perfume of your letter, and it sure felt good for a change to smell something good.

I read your clippings, and it looks like this old world is still marching on. The article about Vietnam is pretty

true. We don't do much moving at all right now. We just sit and wait for them. I've been having all kinds of time up here, as I haven't done a thing for a week now, but sleep and rest. I don't know how long it will last, but it's good while it's lasting. It hasn't rained now for 7 days, and the sun is out and not very hot, in fact, it's better up here than down in base camp.

You ask about my carpenter skills. We busted up an ammo box to build this desk and other things. They have a regular lumber yard down at An Khe that has lots of lumber that we buy to build our buildings. I'm not operating a radio right now. They are going to put me on a switchboard now, I guess.

Well, about 12 choppers just moved in to pick A Company. They are going out on a mission looking for mortars that the Cong has hidden around here. They are also taking four of the German Shepard dogs with them. These dogs are trained to smell out the Cong, just like a bird dog does.

This mountain is not the highest, it just looks like we are up in the clouds when it's foggy and raining. There are about five switchbacks up to it. We've got a lot prettier and better mountains. I'm not sure what the altitude of this mountain is.

Well, I guess my feet are healed up completely now. They weren't very bad anyway; I didn't have to go to bed for them.

That envelope you sent me was all stuck together, so I couldn't use it. I got all kinds of envelopes though. I feel pretty free with my letter writing now that I don't have to put stamps on the envelopes. Well, it's getting to the place where there's not much more to tell. I just lay around in my bunker all day. I suppose before long they will put me to work again.

One thing, I'm making pretty good money over here right now, sending $177.00 to the bank every month. I am up for a promotion this month too. If I get it, that will mean another $60.00 raise.

Well, I better close, I've run out of things to say. So, until I put the press into action again, I am signing off.

Leon

4 Oct 66

Dear Grandma & Grandpa,

Well, I'm in an altogether different type of area now. It's flat and sandy and about 30 degrees hotter. We got to go to base camp just long enough to get supplies, and some guys didn't even get enough time to take a shower. We loaded the trucks at night in the dark and moved out the next morning by truck convoy. The closest village to me now is Bon Song, but by the time you get this letter, I might be somewhere else.

On the mission, we are closing up on the VC and have to move pretty often as this is a search-and-destroy mission. Right now, they got me setting guard all night, and sleeping in the daytime. Sure, is hot weather for October, Ha! Ha!

While writing this letter, I was rudely interrupted by a lizard. He was green and yellow. I was going to bust him with my trenching tool, but he was too fast for me. How is Sparkie's leg? I bet he would have had a fit over the lizard if he could have seen it.

Sounds like Daryl is fixing the place up with all that cement he is putting in. I owe him a letter, but when I'll get time to write, I don't know.

We got two big German Shepard dogs here. They are well-trained dogs. We have some Vietnamese interpreters, and they don't dare wander too close to these dogs or it's all over. Around the villages, they have mutts, just dog rats not good for anything.

You know right now, even the flat lands of Iowa would look better than this place, even if it doesn't have beautiful mountains like Wyoming. They have a lot of wild pigs that run in the jungle. A few of the line companies captured a few, and they look a little on the lien side to me. They sure will bite though. Most of them are all black, although I did see a white pig in a village, so I guess they can be tamed if a person takes the time.

The Captain of our Commo Platoon went and bought a parrot, now that isn't good for anything that I can see.

For now, my home is a whole 6 feet wide, 8 feet long, and 3 feet deep and with a shelter half for a roof. That's pieces of pup tents.

This mission is supposed to last until December 1st, if not longer. I hope I am in base camp for Xmas anyway. Well, won't be long until I have a year in this Army, just a few more days.

I will be moving pretty often, so don't be surprised if my letters start getting fewer and farther in between. I think the Toyne's Press has just about run out of news for today. I got an air mattress now, so when it rains, I can stay on the air mattress and float. I won't drown in the mud like before, pretty soft sleeping too.

Well, till next time. I will bring this to a close for now.

Leon

Leon Toyne now in Vietnam

Army Specialist Fourth Class Leon E. Toyne, 22, son of Mr and Mrs Merritt Toyne, Route 1, Paton, is currently participating in a major operation with the 1st Air Cavalry Division in Vietnam.

Spec. Toyne, a wireman in Headquarters Company, 5th Battalion of the division's 7th Cavalry, and other members of the division are conducting operations in the Central Highlands near Bong Son on the east coast.

During the operation which began October 24, his battalion has thus far killed or captured over 300 Viet Cong and detained more than 800 for questioning.

Large quantities of enemy weapons and food caches have also been captured.

Spec. Toyne entered the Army in October 1965 and arrived in Vietnam in August of this year.

He was graduated from Fremont County Vocational High School, Lander, Wyo., in 1963.

He has been awarded the Combat Infantryman's Badge.

Jefferson Bee, December 12, 1966, Pg 6, Jefferson Iowa

From the Book "The Year of the Horse," when the author Robert Powers arrived in Vietnam in October of 1966 to reinforce the 1st Cavalry Division, 5th Battalion, 7th Cavalry, B Company

Two days later, our orders came, and we were all going in different directions. I was assigned to B Company 5th Battalion, 7th Cavalry, so it was time to say goodbye and good luck to Bob and the other guys that I hung around with.

Rich Roderick drew the same assignment as me, and that eased the pain somewhat. Those of us who were assigned to the 1st Cavalry Division were bused to an airfield and boarded onto a C-130 for a short flight to Camp Ratcliff, the division base camp in An Khe. There were about forty troops on board. We touched down at the base airstrip, grabbed our bags, and offloaded the plane. A sergeant, who was in charge of our group, said that someone would be along to get us and to assemble alongside the tarmac and wait. We watched the C-130 turnaround and took off.

It was raining pretty steadily, and we were soaked. A few minutes later, another C-130 landed and taxied up near where we were grouped. The tailgate went down, and two Air Force crewmen began dragging dead bodies off the plane and lining them up alongside the tarmac. The bodies were wrapped in rain ponchos. The Lifeless, bloody arms and legs were hanging out from the ponchos, and the musty stench of combat infantry permeated the air. It was a shocking and upsetting trip into reality. This was how it was and how it was going to be. This was our introduction to the 1st Cavalry.

The sergeant, our unofficial leader, went over to see if he could help, he was talking to the crew, and they told him that the KIAs were from the 7th Cavalry. Richard and I were very quiet after hearing this. This was the first time in my life that I had seen anything like this, and I'm sure the same was true for Rich. I think it was at this juncture that I convinced myself that I could not let this happen and should not take mental pictures of this horrific scene. I told myself to just keep going forward, do my job, and hope for the best.

Chapter 3: Building Bunkers to Protect from Mortars

9 Oct 66

Dear Grandma & Grandpa,

Well, I got an easy job for a few days. I don't know how long it will last, but I am making good use of it while I got it. There are a dozen of us that moved out on the outside perimeter. There are two of us to a bunker, and we all built real good bunkers so we wouldn't get wet. We are on duty from 6:00 at night till 6:30 in the morning. The rest of the time we sleep and take R&R (rest and relaxation).

We have nice little Vietnamese girls come up to the perimeter fence, and sell us pop, coconuts, and bananas. We go into a nearby village once in a while, and the little kids always want chop, chop, which means food. We always take something in and give it to them. I only wish the rest of the time over here, would be like this mission here so far, but I suppose it will start getting bad before long.

They're chickens running all over the perimeter, and the guy I rode home with, Steve V. and I were trying to catch one to roast, but they fly just like a bird, so we still haven't figured out a way to catch one, as of yet. This kid that road home with Steve V., and I, is John W., he's a machine gunner. He has a jeep with an M-50 machine gun mounted on it, dug in right beside our bunker. Then we got two M-60 machine guns on the other side, so I don't think Charlie Cong has got a chance.

You ask about how the mail works. Well, it's like this. It all comes over by air except those packages weighing over 5 lbs, which have to come by boat. The boat can take a month or more, and Air Mail envelopes have priority over the others. They are sent before the others; therefore, you get the Air Mail letter first. You can just send 5-cent stamps on the letter, and it just takes a little longer before I get it. I know it must be awfully expensive for you, but I sure do enjoy hearing from you. A plane leaves San Francisco every day with the mail. If you want, you can just send 5-cent stamps on letters. I'll still get the mail and that's what counts. It would be a lot cheaper if you would do it that way because 8 cents adds up quicker than it looks. I know I wouldn't write as much if I had to put 8 cents on every letter, but *being free, I decided I might as well take advantage of Uncle Sam as long as I can. You said you sent me a box. For any packages sent by air mail; I have to sign for them. I won't be able to get them until I get back to base camp to sign for it. That might be a month or two.*

Grandpa, these monkeys you asked about are way back in the jungle, and they are wild if you happen to capture one, which is plain luck. They come in all sizes and colors.

Me and old Noseep had a short power nap before we started this next mission. I think the jungle kind of agrees with him, he always comes out looking ready for action.

I heard from someone about Steve Streeter, being over here for an operation, and I bet it was a little hazardous on that ship but as tough as he is he'll probably come out of it in good shape.

It sure doesn't sound like your football team is doing that hot. Also, we don't have lights in our dugouts. The only ones that have them are the Colonels and the big brass.

Well, I ran out of things to say, so this is the Toyne Press going off the air until next time.

Leon.

Leon Toyne in a bunker near An Khe, photo source Leon Toyne family

16 Oct 66

Well, I got kind of lazy today. I slept all day long. I didn't have much else to do today anyway. The weather sure has been dry, as it hasn't rained for a week now. I go without a shirt all day long now, and then in the evening, I have to put a shirt on because the mosquitoes get kind of bad. We put mosquito repellent on when we set guard to keep them from eating us up. We have mosquito nets up where we sleep, so they don't disrupt us when we are sleeping.

I've been told we'll be on this mission until 17 December, so I guess we'll put up a patio, so we can sun ourselves. I have a pretty good sun tan now. I made a washing table yesterday out of two ammo boxes. Then, Nick (Jerry Nicholson), the guy that stays with me in the bunker made an ice box in the ground for our pop. It stays pretty cold too in the wet sand. Nick, use to work in a refrigerator plant, so he knows how to keep things cold pretty well. Me and old Nick have been together on every field problem, we have ever gone on. I met him clear back in Leonardwood. He's a real nice guy.

Don't worry about your letters being boring. I wouldn't care if you told me, it was raining when it should be snowing, it's just the idea of getting a letter from home. Some guys hardly get any letters, and I know they must feel kind of sad when they don't.

Well, you ask about Connie, she's getting along pretty good. That darned old SOB, excuse the language, hasn't got here yet, as he's still in Turkey, says Connie.

Well, not much excitement here lately. Still bringing in VC in large numbers, better than the last mission. They were busy chasing wild hogs instead, last time. I guess they don't have time for that now.

I haven't seen Steve V., I guess he might be back at base camp. We are 60 miles from base camp, so don't know when I'll even get back there, to get your box. All Air Mail packages are classified as registered mail, so still have to sign for it. We are 100 miles from our old mission, so they keep us moving all over the country.

Sounds like Lake City's football team, better hope for a better season next year. Well better bring this to a close.

Leon

Leon Toyne and Jerry Nicholson (Nick) at LZ English, photo source Frank Farrell

24 Oct 66

Dear Grandma & Grandpa,

I received your wonderful box of candy today. The guys that I stand guard with, out here, think I got pretty nice grandparents. John, Chief, Nick, Marty, and I want to let you know it tasted really good.

Well, I worked on my sun tan a little today, and it's drying up again and hasn't rained for two days now. Last week it rained for two days, and two nights pretty steady. We ended up after it was all over, getting three jeeps, four ¾ tons, and six 2 ½ ton trucks stuck in the sand. When it rains so much, there's just no bottom to this ground.

Well, I got my first Vietnamese haircut today, and it's my last. He just trimmed it real light around the edges. Then before I knew it, he gave me a shave, or I guess that's what he called it anyway. He shaved my neck and ears and charged me an extra 50 cents for it. Then the darn little kids tried to shine my shoes. I finally yelled so loud they thought I was going crazy, so they left me alone.

We finished putting up the barbed wire fence on the perimeter. The fence is about 5 feet high, and it's real sharp barbed wire put together in big rolls. It's put down in circles, to make it impossible to cross.

I'm getting used to sleeping about two hours early in the morning, but during the day, it's too hot to sleep, and because the helicopters make too much noise. Right now, I get about five hours of sleep a day.

I did a little trading today. I traded a box of sea rations for a coconut, that's one meal. I guess they raise these coconuts and bananas in the jungle somewhere.

Our line companies sure are looking rough. The guys are losing a lot of weight. They go without eating, so they don't give away their whereabouts to the VC. They get very little sleep too, moving day and night.

Well, I guess I better bring this to a close. Thank you again.   Leon

PS. I got nothing to do again, so I will re-open the press, and write a few more lines. I found out the other day I am living in a graveyard. It gets creepy here at night. There must be a lot of frogs around here because I sure can hear them croaking at night.

I hope you can read this since I'm writing it in the moonlight. We got 18,000 helicopters in Vietnam, and they expect many more by the first of the year. We lose an average of 4-6 a week, from Vietcong shooting them down, or due to power failure.

28 Oct 66

Dear Grandma & Grandpa,

Well, it's 10:30 and I just woke up, nothing to do all day, so I decided I would start out with a letter. This is a real lazy job, and it's safe up to a certain extent, but it's sure boring doing nothing.

I heard we'll be in base camp from 17 Dec to 2 Jan. So, I will get to spend Xmas back where it's fairly safe. Sometimes I think there are more helicopters in Vietnam than there are wheel vehicles. They moved some more in our area on the pad. There must be around 400 to 500 here now. There are still expected to be another 18,000 by January in Vietnam.

You ask about the chickens here. They fly just like pheasants, so I don't know if I'll ever catch a fat one. About a week ago me and this John W. from Iowa captured one in the brushes before it could fly, but it was so skinny and rough looking, so we decided to feed it up. We tied it to the jeep and fed it a few C-rations, then that night a dog found it, and chewed her up pretty bad, so we turned it loose.

Say, Grandpa, I was beginning to wonder, has Lake City won any football games this year at all? The players must be pretty green at it, or small.

Well, it looks like starting in January we will pull perimeter guard 3 months in the towers around the base camp. Then they say we would go out on one big long mission, then it will be time to rotate back to the states. I only hope I get another easy job like this one on my last mission. The way our line companies have been getting shot up, I might have to go out with the line companies along with some of the rest of headquarters. Our job is to support the line companies. A lot of the ones that have been brought in are suffering from heat stroke, or merge foot, which is what I had on the mountain.

You ask about Billy T. I've been getting a lot of letters from him lately. He's still going to some type of school, and he's afraid they will extend him because it will take about two years of schooling before they can use him.

I suppose you will be getting snow before long. I guess I won't see any snow this year, still hot as ever.

Grandma, how're your wild women? Sounds like they take off on you, but don't get far. I was always told women aren't quite as smart as a man, Ha! Ha!

I got a letter from Daryl & Barbara. They sure must be working hard and sounds like they are really fixing their places up. I guess he's starting on his corn now.

Well, I have no further traffic at this time, so this is a roger out. In case you want to know, that's RTO talk.

Leon

Chapter 4: Phu Cat – Friendly Villagers

29 Oct 66

Dear Grandma & Grandpa,

Shucks, I haven't got a thing to do, and cannot find anything to do, so decided to open up the old press again. Before I forget to tell you, I really like those jokes you send with your letters.

Well, I'll try and make a letter out of this. I don't know too much to tell you, due to the press hasn't gathered up too much information since I wrote last, but we'll try and find a few pages.

This place we are operating at this month is going to be a permanent camp, and someday, be a regular Army base here I suppose. They are building all kinds of roads and leveling the land to spread out the camp bigger and make room for the helicopters. Some of the areas are blacktopping.

We got a PX out here now, so it's just about like base camp. The nearest Vietnamese village is Phu Cat, which is about five miles from here. You look at this place from a distance it looks like a bunch of ants building a home. One side is all flat and sandy, and the other is high mountains with a lot of vegetation. We also have big machines just like you see on construction crews for building roads.

Got a letter from the Dials, and they said everyone is busy picking corn. I only wish I was driving a tractor instead of a mule, but that's the way the ball bounces, as Dad would say.

I guess I won't mind these two years so bad if I get out of here in the same shape as I went in.

The big wheels keep telling us that this is a tour over here and we are guests in this country and we are to treat these people as such, darn if I don't find that hard to believe.

I got your letter from Daryl's girls. I rea enjoy them. That Chris sure can write interesting letters. I would write to them, but I don't know what to write to little girls. I have a hard time writing to my brothers. But you tell them I got their letters, and I might figure out something to write back before

I leave here. One thing for sure on this mission, I've had more time to write than I did back in the states.

These mosquitoes are just as big as your mosquitoes. I use repellent on them at night, so they get pretty sick after they bite me.

It might be funny, but on these packages, I always get the plain ones before I get the air mail ones, I still haven't figured that one out. I got a package from Mom & Dad that wasn't airmailed, I got it in a week.

Grandpa, sure glad to hear Lake City finally won a game, for a while I thought they were duds too. Well, no, or fewer turnover this time. The press will rest till next time.

Roger Out. RTO Talk.

Leon

5 Nov 66

Dear Grandma and Grandpa,

I received your package that was sent on 29 Sep. I got it on the 1st of November. I hate to tell you this, but I know you worked so hard baking the candy, but it was all moldy. The cookies, peanuts, shaving cream, and soap

wasn't hurt a bit. At one time the package must have gotten wet because you could tell where the water had been on the box. I did enjoy all the rest of it anyway.

Well, here it is Nov and I'm right back where I started from. We moved back to where our bunkers were, the day before we started to move. It rained as usual, so I had a wet bed that night. This time we built a complete

wooden bunker, with a wood floor and everything. The only thing that isn't wood is the canvas roof. I guess it was time for us to leave our new position anyway. Because early that day we killed two snakes, one was five feet long. He was just a little way outside our bunker and gear. The other one was only two and one-half feet long. I don't think they were poison, but I didn't investigate the matter.

We were taking our bunker down and everybody was getting ready to move out when these people that were staying in the village near us, came over and started to take our lumber. They started to overrun us, and take everything, but Old Chief, a kid in the bunker next to ours, picked up the five-foot snake and took after the people with it. One of the old girls grabbed one of our best blankets and started to run when Chief came with the snake. I ran after her, but she got away and I thought I better get back and guard what we had left. Old Chief went to eat supper while the rest of us kept hauling our bunkers and gear. When he got back, they had taken everything he had. There wasn't a thing left where his bunker was standing.

Whenever an outfit moves out, whatever they leave behind doesn't stay there long. Nick was over getting flares and wires from an old ration case, and there were a few C-Rations left. About a dozen kids were standing by him while he was getting the flares out. Before he could get away, the kids had knocked him over to get into the box. They were fighting and yelling, some of the craziest language you had ever heard.

You ask about fruit. They have bananas and pineapple and that's about all the fruit I've seen. Sure got a lot of onions and sweet potato patches all around our bunker.

As far as their language goes, it's pretty hard to understand. I know this much, if you want them to go and leave you alone, you say "DD", and they start running. We have an Old Papa San out in front of our bunker he's a pretty friendly old boy. He helped us put up the wire, and build one of the bunkers right in one of the sweet potato patches, and he never even got mad. We give him cigarettes all the time, so he kind of thinks we're even, I guess.

Pour ole Noseep, I saw his name on the hospital roster. He can't see out of his left eye; he's just about lost all of his vision out of it. At least he's getting some rest. Those troops that have been running through the jungle look pretty beat. Most of our trouble is merge feet. In the camp we got here, about 100 troops are running around with no shoes, so their feet will heal up. I'll try and get Noseep's serial number for you. It's sure a poor way to get clean sheets and a bed to sleep in.

Well, I guess I'll visit you some more. This will be the second day of this letter, and it looks like it's really to be a whopper before I get it finished.

Well, today we winterized our home. We put tar paper on the outside and put dirt up against it and built a front porch. Now I think we have a better place to live than we had back at the base camp. We had a lot of help, but we haven't got the fence fixed yet, so the kids keep coming over. We had six boys here from ages 5 to 10 years, I would guess. They helped us dig dirt and carry sandbags. One of them can count to 60. I know because he counted *the sandbags. Then he counted a bunch of nails we had. I don't know where he learned it, but he's pretty smart. We gave them each a package of gum after they had finished helping us. The only problem is when one comes, then the whole village starts coming, so we have to run them back when there are too many. I'll kind of be glad when we get the fence up. They get to be a nuisance at times. You have to watch them or they will steal your stuff, so one guy has to be at the bunker all the time.*

We don't have a problem getting our clothes washed now. Moma San does it. I guess you might say we have it real soft. We also have our own lumber yard and plenty of material to work from. There's an ammo dump right next to us, and they throw all the ammo boxes and crates in a hole, so we help ourselves.

I'm sending you a little piece of paper that the VC throw out of a helicopter when we capture them. In the front where the picture is the VC beating and killing the peaceful villagers. The back is some Vietnamese language, I don't understand it.

I guess I better bring this whopper of a letter to a close. Say, I bet you'll never guess what I'm doing tonight. Nick got a package from his parents. He got a sack of marshmallows and were roasting them over a candle. They sure are good.

We put bamboo shutters on our bunker for windows, so when we want to look out, we just pull a string, and they raise up. Keeps the sun out and peeping Toms.

Well, I better close the press. I have to let her rest after putting out such a letter.

Leon

VC Propaganda thrown from helicopters, after capture (front), source Leon Toyne family

VC Propaganda thrown from helicopters, after capture (back), source Leon Toyne family

6 Nov 66

Dear Grandma & Grandpa,

I received your most welcome letter, and I thoroughly enjoyed the newspaper you sent me about the article on the Split-Rock ranch round-up. I went to school with that one kid, and I know his dad fairly well. Almost went to work out there one time.

Well, you ask about my pets, well I haven't got any since I turned my chicken loose. I'm not far enough out in the jungle to have any monkeys, and not too many alligators get in my way either. The snakes, I'm always running them around the onion patch.

You ask if there's anything I need. Well, there is a couple of things. A small scrub brush to wash my clothes out by hand. Then I sure could use a hair brush to scratch my head with. I have a comb, but it doesn't seem to get the job done. There also are the cigars, which I smoke quite a few of them. I've been getting a day's worth of tobacco plugs in my rations, but I swallowed some a few days ago, so I don't care for it anymore. When you are out on patrol, you can't smoke. I know one thing, I'm sure not going to swallow tobacco anymore for a while. If I even smell it now, my belly was wild. That's all I need, for now, I guess.

Grandpa, glad to hear Lake City won another game. I guess the football season is almost over now. Maybe your basketball team will make up for having a little slow football team.

So, Kermit thinks Mike's a pretty good hand. I guess Mike will never have any trouble getting a job.

You say you have been sending newspapers, well I haven't seen any. They could be coming by boat due to so much mail. I don't think they are holding any packages back at base camp anymore, because I did get two; one from you and one from Grandma Mantz.

There sure getting to be a lot of dogs around here. Seems like everyone around here in the main camp has a little dog. I guess they buy them from the villagers. How is Sparkie getting along? I bet he doesn't care much for that cold weather. What about the wild women at the prison? Does that weather make them feisty?

Well, the old press doesn't have much to tell, so I'll just visit along here. When I set guard at night I think about home and wonder what everyone is doing. One thing doing nothing, a person has a lot of time to think. I'm still wondering whether to be a flatland farmer or a Wyoming cowboy. I guess I'll know one way or another when I get out. I still have 269 days to make up my mind. I sure wish I was there to plow up those corn stalks for Daryl, that's kind of fun. Just might have to load up my ole cow pony and spend a little while with you all.

Well, here it is another day, and I still haven't finished this letter. I got a newspaper from you today. The date on it is October 22nd, so I guess they are still coming through. Woke up at 1100 this morning, so it felt pretty good. I'm getting so I can sleep a little bit in the daytime now.

I guess I'll close the old press down, don't have much more to say, but wanted to write a few lines anyway.

P.S. Thanks for the paper.

Leon

10 Nov 66

Dear Grandma & Grandpa,

I received your most welcome letter a few days ago, so will try and write a few lines this morning. Well, yesterday we were trying out a new invention. We took a casing that 105 shells came in, and buried it in the ground. Then we put it half full of sand. We got some JP4 helicopter fuel and poured the casing full. Then we put a plastic cover over it to keep the rain out. Next, we tied a trip flare to a stake and then drove it down over the casing, with the flare upside down. Lastly, we ran some Commo wire to our bunker to trip it. Talk about something lighting up the place at night, that does. We pull the trip wire, the flare burns through, the plastic ignites the fuel, and really lights up our area. We only use them when vision is very poor. Frankenstein hasn't got anything on us, Ha! Ha!

You ask what SP4 is; it's the same as corporal. I sure hope my orders hurry up and get down, so I'm making that extra $60 a month.

You mention the helicopters. They are the main means of transportation out here. They carry all of the supplies, chow, and anything you can think of to the line companies. We even have helicopters that act as ambulances you might say. As soon as someone gets hit, they call for a helicopter on the radio, and the person is evacuated in a matter of minutes. Another time I have seen one carry a road grader the other day, so they can carry anything. When someone gets shot down another one comes in and picks him up.

Grandpa, you ask about the price of bananas over here. Well, they don't cost anything, if you want to climb a tree and get them. They are really small and have quite a few seeds in them, but they taste pretty good. You also ask about Vietnamese, a person picks up some of the languages, but a lot of it's pretty difficult to say. Some of those girls are really sharp looking too.

As for how many of our outfits are here. Well, where I am there's only a headquarters company, which is about 175 guys. We have guys coming in all the time from the line companies, so right now, I suppose there are about 250 in our outfit, but their other outfits all around us. This camp we are in is the 9th Army, and they're supposed to take it over. Altogether, with all the outfits in this area, there must be close to 1200 troops. We have 4 Line companies in our outfit. They are A, B, C, and D Companies. Our A company has 4 platoons with 40 to 50 to a platoon. The other companies have just 3 platoons. We are already getting a lot of replacements coming in. In Our Commo section alone we got five. The line companies got over 100, of course, they have lost a lot of guys.

This weather has changed for the last two or three days. The sun hardly ever comes out, so it's been pretty cool and nice.

Well, I suppose everyone has all the corn picked by now. After that's done, and they cannot plow, I suppose they take it easy the rest of the winter.

Well, guess I better bring this to a close. Cannot think of anything to say right now.

Leon

Chapter 5: Papa San

15 Nov 66

Dear, Grandma & Grandpa,

Well, here I am again, so decided to write you a few lines, nothing to do but write a letter or two. One thing is for sure, this is the first time I ever stayed caught up on my letter writing.

Well, I got some good news and some bad news. I'll tell you the good news first. I made SP4 so I'm no PFC anymore. I also get a pay raise along with that, so I feel pretty good about that part of it. Now, for the bad news. There's a good chance I'll be extended 3 to 5 months. Probably to train new troops back in the states I imagine.

Say, have you ever eaten sugar cane? I'm pretty friendly with an Old Papa San, he gives me a chunk now and then. It sure tastes juicy.

I received your big bundle of newspapers on the 6th of November. I'm still reading them, a lot of interesting news in them. I enjoy the funnies extra well because we don't get a very good funny paper out here.

So, you dig those crazy envelopes, do you? I got 72 of them, so you might see a few more before I run out. Since I have been over here, I have used up a little over 100 envelopes, so you know I must write a few letters. I write quite a few of them to Wyoming also.

You ask about our mules. The only gun on them is the one you carry when you get on it. The gun is a part of me for now. Wherever I go, it goes. It's never very far from me at any time. We use our mules a lot to haul supplies to the helicopter pad to be loaded. We do everything possible with them, and sometimes things are impossible.

One day we hooked two mules to a jeep to pull it out of the mud hole. The jeeps are pretty light. One person can pick one up and tip it over. It'd sure be the thing to have on a ranch.

Tell Sparkie, thanks for the gum, it was really good. Say, I saw something you don't see every day. I saw a monkey chasing a dog. The poor old dog didn't know what the fuzzy creature was.

I got a little business going hear on the side. I buy jungle hats from Papa San for $1.50 and sell them to the guys for $2.00. It's something to pass the time. Marty buys mirrors from him and sells them for a profit too. If I can

find a way, I'm going to send two hats home to Steve and Mike. I got to find a box to fit them into first, which is a problem where I'm at, but I'll get them sent one of these days before I rotate.

You ask about deer. They don't have any deer, but they have water buffaloes. Then there's something else that's strange, their cattle don't ball, or make a sound. Maybe they disconnected the voice box on them. Ha! Ha!

Sounds like those women at the reformatory really can bring the smoke. Sounds like you handled the combat situation perfectly.

Well, I guess I better bring this to a close. The press will rest until next time.

Leon.

15 Nov 66 (Part 2)

Dear Grandma & Grandpa,

Well, I will write a few lines in answer to your most welcome letters, and to thank you for the Kool-Aid, and newspapers I received a few days ago. Well, today finds me doing nothing again, as usual. Not too much to write about it seems anymore.

They restocked the PX today. Had two 2 ½ ton trucks full of pop, and they sold it all in two days. When the PX gets supplies in, they usually buy them out in one day. They had a line a half mile long waiting to buy something. Seems like whenever you want to buy something, you have to wait in lines to get it, if they haven't already sold out.

Well, here it is another day, and I still haven't finished this letter. I got KP Saturday, and it sure doesn't make me happy. I think I would rather dig a hole than mess around with those old pots & pans. The ole mess hall sergeant and I don't get along anyway. He looks like an old bulldog.

Last night, Nick, Chief, and I had four good games of rummy. It started to get hot so we opened the windows, and pretty soon it started to rain. All of a sudden, little frogs started jumping through the window on our card table. Man, they were jumping everywhere all over the place. We had to hold the game up to run the frogs off.

Grandpa, I told you there wasn't any deer out here. Well, I was talking to Papa San, and he said there are a lot over by An Khe, our base camp.

It sure must keep you busy writing and sending me things all the time. I want you to know I sure do enjoy it. The only thing to look forward to is a mail call.

Well, I guess I'm going to be interrupted again. The rummy game is getting ready to get underway again. I'll get this letter finished before the end of the month anyway, Ha! Ha! It's raining anyway, so it's a good time to play. I received your letter that was written on the 10th, only five days, that's a pretty good time.

You ask about the Vietnamese liking us. Well, they like you until your back is turned, then they'll rob you blind. Mom sent me a new pen, and they took it when I went to chow. They took some things from Nick too. Mom sent that pen in a regular envelope. I wonder if you could send me one in a regular envelope and that way it won't

take very long to get here. This pen I'm using now doesn't write most of the time.

You ask about vegetables. We get carrots, olives, apples and oranges for fruit. We get quite a bit of good food. I haven't received the package yet, but due to Xmas, there's probably a lot of mail to take care of.

They are starting a new mission up North, so I suppose Steve S. is up there. I hear all that happens out there. I'm sure Steve is all right. He knows how to take care of himself pretty well.

I sure do enjoy hearing from you. A letter a day makes me a good boy or something like that. Well, here I am at the bottom of the page, so I guess I'll close the press till next time.

Leon

20 Nov 66

Dear Grandma & Grandpa,

I'll try and think of a few lines to write in answer to your most welcome letters, and thank you for the box of candy, if I didn't in my first letter. I also got a letter from Christine today, so I need to take some time, and try and think of a few lines to write that nice little girl. She sure is a good letter writer. I also got the other letters with yours. I really enjoyed them all.

Sure, sounds like a prisoner has an easy life, but I suppose not, but easy in some ways. Out here these people would think a bowling ball is some kind of ammunition for a cannon or something. Say, I sure remember when I beat you, Grandma. I beat you didn't I, wow! We will have to try again after I get you a little more practice. I'll try not to beat you too badly next time.

Well, old Noseep somewhat lucked out, and a tough way to do it. He was no good in combat anymore, with that bad eye, so they stationed him in Japan, so he doesn't have a thing to worry about anymore.

Sounds like Daryl is going to raise a lot of corn and beans next year. I bet he could use a good hand.

I sure have a lot of time to write, but I can't think of anything to write. I suppose after the mission they will really put me to work. I guess we have to lay a lot of wire back at base camp. When I said I was back where I started, I meant that old area I was guarding, Bon Song. If you wondered what BS means.

This month must be harvest time because villagers are cutting their rice paddies. They cut it and haul it after it dries on a stick, tied in a bundle across their shoulder. They pound it again to knock the rice out of the stocks. Then they spread the rice on a hard surface, and roll the hulls of rice, and from there I don't know what they do. They cut it out of the paddy with a small knife like this poor drawing of a curved knife, like a very small sickle.

I guess we would call them very hard workers. They go from daylight to dark. They all work. The kids carry little bundles and the older ones, are the bigger bundles.

Well, guess I better close till next time, as the old press isn't in too good of shape for news.

Leon

P.S. Well here it is broken down in plain English, DD means (get the hell out of here!)

Grandpa, you think your old press isn't working too hot Man! Mine's worn so bad it wobbles when I write. I want to thank you and Sparkie for the present.

I did go to the dentist today and got a tooth filled. That's all I've got done today, and it looks like I have about four more to get filled. I sure do hate to go there, but I've found out it's worse if I wait.

Seems like the days are going pretty fast out here. That helps a little bit, but still, a person gets tired of doing nothing. This Army life sure makes a person lazy. Well by the time you get this letter, November will be just about gone. Do you have any snow back there yet?

24 Nov 66

GOT MY PRESS FIXED!

Dear Grandma & Grandpa,

I received your most welcome letter today. Cannot find anything to do right now. So, I decided I might have a little visit with the flat land people, and find out how things are on the other side of the world.

We are getting ready to move out and go back to An Khe on the 1st of December. I probably won't be writing as often as I have been. So, I guess I'll be leaving this nice little house before long.

Say you asked how the bananas tasted. Well, pretty bitter, and lots of seeds in them too. Tastes a little green. The closest village here is Phu Cat, which is four miles from where I'm at. This is about 185 miles from Saigon.

Say, I sure wish I could sell these letters for $1000, don't know of anybody who would be in the market to pay that, would you? I would settle for just ¼ of the $1000 JP flares being used only when we are being attacked when it happens. We tripped one off the other day to see how it would work. It burned about 4 hours before it went out.

Sure was nice of you all to send me the brushes and things. I already got Barbara's package, so will probably get the brushes for a long. It sure was a good cake she made. Got here in less than two weeks.

My feet are in pretty good shape now. I found out what one of the problems was, and that was wearing wool socks. They seem to make my feet break out. Bill's mother sent some others and I've been trying them. I think that will take care of some of the trouble.

Well, let's see what else I can think of to write about. Sure, sorry to hear Daryl is having trouble with his calves. Sure does need a good cowhand to look over them for him. How many head did he buy this year? Are they

Herefords? Must be the change of feed to make them scour. Don't know too much about Minnesota cattle though. I came from what you call one of the better cattle countries where the cattle stay pretty healthy if they got a good cowpuncher to look after them. But here I am wasting my valuable experience wet nursing a bunch of no-good nesters. What a way for a cowboy to live. Ride iron mules, and chew sugar cane. Things sure should look a lot different next fall, or they <u>will</u> look different. Get rid of that old baggy uniform for good. Well, now you know how I feel about the whole situation.

Got a feeling this letter won't be worth quite $1000.00, due to not much interesting news, but that's the way it goes when you do nothing to write about.

Say you mentioned Steve, he sure is getting tall, they sent me those school pictures. There sure is a difference between Steve and Mike, just like night and day. Steve's more like me, but Mike, I don't know whom he takes after. Mike's pretty smart, he might not have to work for a living. He will probably get one of those desk jobs, a white-collar worker.

I got your newspaper, and lemonade a few days ago. Quite an article on the Mack family, a long time to live without a woman. I don't know if I could hold out that long. I think I'll do a lot of shopping before I put my brand on any young filly. She sure will have to have a good bloodline, and maybe a little money, Ha!

Well, this may be kind of a crazy mixed-up letter, but I didn't have anything to do. I like to keep the ink warm in my press anyway.

Well, happy trails till we visit again. Closing with my livestock brand!

Leon

Leon Toyne's Wyoming livestock brand "quarter circle broken arrow"

Toyne Ranch putting the "quarter circle broken arrow" brand on calves on Gooseberry Creek

29 Nov 66

Dear Grandma & Grandpa,

I received your most welcome packages today, which were sent on the 21st, only eight days, that's a remarkable time. I sure don't know how to ever thank you; you sure do take good care of me. Sending me all these good things. I have already tried out the scrub brush, sure beats paying old Papa San 50 cents to do my fatigues, when I have a lot of time to do them myself.

Someday I'll find a way to express my thanks a little better when I'm home where it's safe. That chewing tobacco keeps me on my toes when I'm setting a guard.

Well, let's see what's happened since I wrote you last. It rained for five days and five nights. It finely let up today. Got 18 inches in two days, so you figure it rained pretty hard. The old bunker didn't float away, but it came darn close. We had a few minor leaks, but never got too wet.

The village kids are getting friendly again. There was a bunch of them down in the bunker, eighteen in the main bunker. There were some little girls, and one of them was going through the other one's hair picking out bugs, and eating them. I didn't believe it until I watched it for a while, and sure enough, she was eating lice bugs.

Some of them wash pretty well, but others don't believe in baths, I guess.

About the packages again, you must have really chewed out the guy that carried the mail and sorted it. What did you do to that poor man? They must have heard my Grandparents don't like them getting my mail wet, and losing it. Well, you must have him worried anyway, so shouldn't have any more trouble with him for a while, Ha! Ha!

Well, our Battalion Commander is sick and got some bad disease, so they're shipping him back to the states. Don't know who will take over our battalion now. Things will probably start changing around here now.

Well, we were going back to An Khe on the 1st of December, but doesn't look like we'll make it now. All the bridges got washed out from the big rain, so got to wait until they get them back in. We now will go back by truck convoy.

The magazine you sent, sure has a big line of machinery, that must be why you don't find too many rich farmers because they invest all the money in machinery. I guess the horsepower days are gone for sure in your country.

Well, I got eight more months over here. We rotate from here in July, and I'll sure be glad when that comes. I guess everyone else is counting the days just like me. It sure is something to look forward to.

How is everyone back there? Have you got any snow yet? Are the wild women getting any wilder? How about Lake City's basketball team, how are they coming along by now? How many games have they won so far?

Well, can't think of anything to write, so will try and see if I can do better when we move out of here. We should have the bridges in 3 or 4 days.

I want to thank you for the packages. That brush you thought was too big, I'll find something to use it on, as it will come in handy later on.

Leon

2 Dec 66

Dear Grandma & Grandpa,

I received your two most welcome letters yesterday, and the fruit cake today, also got the paper and gum. So, you might say I'm getting my mail in real good shape.

Still raining here. Been pretty cool, and windy this week. You ask about old Papa San's sweet potatoes. Well, they are growing taller every day. They have a long stem, which is about a ½ inch thick, with little leaves at the top. Some of these plants grow taller than six feet. Whenever he gets hungry, he just goes out and pulls a few. Nick ate supper with him one night. He said he had onions, rice, crushed peanuts, and coffee. They eat just twice a day. Rice is their main diet.

Well, you asked about being SP4. That doesn't change your job, it just gives me a little more responsibility, and you can give a few orders to those under you. You mentioned Steve V. His camp is in the same place as mine.

I know, going without a bath for 30 days is a long time, but I did it when we were in the mountains guarding highway 19, wow! A person gets pretty raunchy, but one guy smells just as bad as the other, you know you're not the only one that smells. Darn luck, the shower point here is about two miles from our bunker. I just get on the mule and go whenever I want. Go every day sometimes.

Say, Grandpa did you pick out these cigars? They sure are good, in fact, I got a cloud of smoke going right now. You got a good eye for cigars.

You mention going back to Iowa and living with you. You wouldn't want me; you've always seen my good side. Wow! When I get mad, or something doesn't go just right, I'm a bearcat. Ask my folks, they know. But I imagine before this is over, Iowa will probably be my home, because that's where my family lives.

Say, about that fruit cake, boy, that sure was a whopper. It was nice and fresh, and extra good. Don't know how I'll ever repay you for all those nice things you send.

In our headquarters company, they are getting overstocked with men, so they are transferring them to the 1st CAV because most of their guys are rotating home. They take so many each month, I suppose. I'll be going over there before long. A lot of my old buddies are all already over there now, so I won't be with strangers when I do go.

Let's see what else I know. Oh, I don't think they will extend me after all, they put out some new information saying, anyone putting 12 months in Vietnam wouldn't be extended most likely. So, I still might get out early, sure counting on it.

You mention Lake City not going to win a basketball game when they play Churdan. Churdan must have a pretty good team. How do you think they will do at the state tournament? I suppose it's too early to tell though.

Well can't seem to think of anything worth writing, so will close the old press down until next time.

Thank you for the cake, not a crumb was wasted.

Leon

4 Dec 66

Dear Grandma & Grandpa,

I received your most welcome letter with the pen in it yesterday. Just a few days after I received the package with the other two pens, so I got plenty of pens now. The one you sent in the letter sure is an expensive one. You didn't have to get one so good. I sure like it anyway and it writes just great.

About the PX. I waited till the next day when there was no line. When the line companies are in for a rest, or to get re-supplied. About that old bulldog-looking mess hall sergeant I got. I just cuss him and give him dirty looks and gripe about the rotten chow he puts out, to make him a little madder. When I have KP he stays out of my way, and it seems to work out pretty well that way. If I ever make sergeant, which will be just before my estimated time of separation (ETS) comes up. I'll bring some smoke on that old grumpy sergeant for a few days.

You mention boring letters, no letter is boring to me, even if it says It's raining and getting wet. When mail call comes, that's the fastest I move all day. I'll travel a long way to get a letter.

The NVA/VC sure are shooting down a lot of our helicopters this last week. We had six wrecked ones sitting out here, where they fuel and load supplies on them. That's about 4 ½ million dollars' worth of aircraft. They bring in the wrecked ones for parts for some of the others, and to prevent the VC from taking the radios out of them, and other useful things.

Well, here I am again. I will try and finish this letter this time. I had quite a little excitement a few minutes ago. Mike and I were down by bunker 18, guarding the bunkers, while the other guys went to chow. All of sudden we saw this big kid sneaking up to my bunker. So, we took in after him. Mike went one way and me the other. I was jumping barbed wire, running through brush and jungle like that roadrunner you see in the cartoons. We got him cornered, but he never had time to steal anything. So, we couldn't do much for him. When we left, he was shaking pretty badly, so I guess we did some good.

Well, I got KP again Wednesday, so I have to watch out for that old bulldog-faced sergeant. It'll just be dirty looks, and think to myself what I'd like to do to him.

When it gets dark and we can't see at all on guard, we shoot off flares. That lights up the area for about 40 seconds. I shot one off the other night and hit it with the side of my hand, sure sore, so I guess that's a good excuse for my handwriting. You sure have to hold your arm steady, because those flares got a pretty big kick to them, and they can sprain your wrist if you relax. I heard one kid over in another company, shot or burned I should say, a hole through the roof of his bunker.

Well, I'll bring this boring letter to a close.

Leon

Taken from the 31 July 1967 Command Health Report Memo for the month of June 1967, the 5th Battalion (Air Mobile), 7th Cavalry. Courtesy of National Archives, College Station, Maryland

The Vietnam troops received numerous shots to protect them from the diseases associated with working in the jungles of

Vietnam. The following shots were checked for in the troop's records for the June 1966 audit. Malaria was not listed in the memo, which was also given to troops when they first arrived in Vietnam in tablet form.

A records check of 800 records revealed that 94% of the records were current for the following shots: *Smallpox, Typhoid, Typhus, Cholera, Plague, Influenza, Polio, and Others.*

11 Dec 66

Dear Grandma and Grandpa,

Well, I moved back to base camp on the 7th, and they have been working with me. We've been laying wire lines

from daylight to dark and should finish in a day or so. I've sure been doing a lot of pole-climbing trees, trying to get the wires off the ground. Then they got us to clean up the equipment. Didn't feel too good today, had to get six shots. Wow, are my arms ever sore.

I saw Steve V. today. He looks pretty good after what he's been through. A <u>medic</u> has a pretty big and rough job over here.

I sure hated to leave ole Papa San and that easy job. He gave us a little party for us the day we left. We had coffee, pop, and beer. Then we played cards, or he did. They got some kind of game where they just use the cards 9 through Ace. They gamble too, just like people back in the states where they play poker for money. The two nice-looking village girls sure hated to see us go. They had a few tears in their eyes.

We came back to base camp in a truck convoy. It sure was a long old rough ride. We had to wait for them to put a bridge in, that was washed out.

Well, you'll never guess what they are going to have me doing now. I am operating a switchboard. Starting Monday, I'll be pulling about eight hours a day on it. I don't much care for it, but it's better than KP by a long shot. I guess we'll be staying in camp till January 5th.

I got your newspaper a few days ago, along with the candy. I also got the nice crisp cookies too, so the mail is coming in good shape. I got the Christmas card too. You mentioned buying books. You didn't have to do that. You already have got me enough presents. I sure want to thank you for all of them too.

I got another little favor I want to ask you to do. My 66-pocket calendar is almost gone. I need a new 67 so I can keep marking the days off. It's just one of those small kinds that you can carry in your billfold. If you find one, I sure would like it.

You ask if they have any wild game birds. I haven't seen anything but parrots, and there sure are a lot of them around here, seems like every section in the battalion has one. We got a green and yellow one in the Commo platoon.

This new pen you sent me sure works great, and the only time it stops is when the lights go out. They just went out a few minutes ago. I guess the generator ran out of gas, and all these lights are run by big gas generators.

You mentioned Sparkie getting cold. This sure would be a good place for him. It's hotter than the devil over here, but rains every day, so that cools a person off some.

Well, I'm on the end of the page, so better close the press. Don't be worried if you don't get many letters from me for a while, because we are really busy.

Leon

Chapter 6: Doc Vincent and Bravo Company

Steve "Doc" Vincent with his non-issue M-16, photo source Steve Vincent's family

News from servicemen, Des Moines Register paper December 29, 1965.

Pvt Steven E. Vincent, 19, son of Mr. and Mrs. Carl L. Vincent, Route 1, Lake City, IA, and Pvt Steven Streeter, 20, son of Mr. and Mrs. Russell M. Streeter, Route 2, Lake City, IA, are attending a medical aidman course at the Army Medical Training Center, Fort Sam Houston, Texas. During the 10-week course, which began December 15, Vincent and Streeter are receiving instruction in the application of medical treatment, with emphasis on the care of battlefield casualties.

They entered the Army in September 1965 and completed basic training at Fort Leonardwood, Missouri. Vincent graduated from Lake City High School in 1964 and was employed by Quarter Oats Co., Rockwell City, before entering the Army. Streeter is a 1963 graduate of West View High School and was engaged in farming before entering the Army.

Article from Des Moines Register, December 29, 1965.

Pvt. Steven Vincent, Pvt. Steven Streeter and a young man from Carnarvon escaped injury when the car they were returning to Fort Sam Houston, Texas, burned up near Junction City, Kansas, at about 1030 a.m., Tuesday, December 28.

Vincent, who owned the car, was asleep in the back seat when he was awakened by heat on his shoulder.

He called to Streeter, who was driving, to pull off the road. The boys escaped from the car before it burst into flames, but lost practically all their possessions.

The three are in medical training with the U.S. Army at Fort Sam Houston, Texas. The parents of the Lake City servicemen are Mr. And Mrs. Carl Vincent and Mr. and Mrs. Russell Streeter.

Comments from interviewing Gene and Loa Dawn Vincent: "Steve wasn't issued an M-16 as a medic; standard weapon issue for combat medics was a .45 Caliber pistol. Steve said his job was to help save lives, but he wanted to protect lives too, and taking on the VC with a .45 pistol against their rifles was insane. So, Steve acquired an M-16 through unauthorized channels, which cost him a stripe. He said that it was worth it because the M-16 saved his life. Oh, by the way, he did earn that stripe back."

Information for the Vietnam War, Obtained from the National Archives, College Park, Maryland.

Over the course of the war in Vietnam, 303,704 Americans were wounded as a result of enemy action. Of this number, those losing at least one limb totaled more than all those in WWII and Korea combined. Almost one-third of those wounded in Vietnam came home with a permanent physical disability.

It could have been worse if not for the efficient and timely treatment afforded by the field medics and corpsmen. The speedy evacuation, normally by helicopter, and the advanced medical services provided in the rear area hospitals, 82 percent of those wounded in action survived. In comparison to wars in the past, this number was remarkable.

WHAT IT WAS REALLY LIKE AS A MEDIC IN THE VIETNAM WAR Read More:

https://www.grunge.com/321306/what-it-was-really-like-as-a-medic-in-the-vietnam- war/?utmcampaign=clip

The combat medic is a unique type of soldier, putting themselves in the middle of a life-threatening battle, but they do so in order to save, not take lives. Not only must they work with limited resources to save lives, but they must also do so under intense pressure, knowing that their own lives could come to an end at any moment.

To put it bluntly, it's a job that requires nothing short of nerves of steel. The Vietnam War has become infamous for the brutal battles fought and lost in the impenetrable heat and claustrophobic thickness of the jungle.

Following American soldiers into the line of fire, hoping to prevent them from becoming yet more casualties, were their medics.

Medics trained alongside other troops, but their job in the field was to patch up their comrades when the bullet, grenade, or shell with their name on it found its target. Without body armor or even bulletproof helmets, medics were in as much danger as their comrades and sometimes more. While soldiers could hunker down during bombardments, the medic ran towards the enemy to find the wounded, often with little more than a few bandages, some morphine, a pair of blunt scissors, and little to no medical training.

Even when the guns were silent, medics were in charge of soldiers' general health, treating them for diseases from malaria to foot rot. This is what it was really like as a medic in the Vietnam War.

The following excerpt was taken from the book "1966 The Year of the Horse," written by Robert K Powers, an Army infantryman from 1st Air Division (Air Mobile) 5th Battalion, 7th Cavalry, Bravo Company, where Steve "Doc" Vincent was their combat medic during 1966-1967.

Mail was probably the single most important thing to a grunt in the field. It was like a ray of sunshine or a glimmer of hope that we all desperately needed. When one of your buddies drew a blank at mail call, the disappointment in his eyes told the story. It would be followed by a moment of silence, and if you got mail, you knew better than to flaunt it or say much. I was extremely fortunate that I had so many people writing to me, but some of the guys only occasionally got a letter.

Steve "Doc" Vincent came up with a cure for the mail malady. Somehow, he had gotten hold of a list of potential pen pals in the States, and he passed them along to anyone interested. This turned out to be a real morale builder. Now we all had something to look forward to, especially those guys that received very little mail.

I wouldn't say I was glad to be in the country, but I wouldn't want to be with any other guys. They were a perfect melting pot of the States. Each of them had a completely different background, and that always made for interesting conversation. Doc Vincent was a farm boy from Iowa. He was a husky kid with a big shock of curly red hair and an impish smile. He would tell me I had a nice neck, and he was looking forward to doing a tracheotomy on me. He had that kind of humor, but he would be the first guy to lend a hand. He was a medic, but when the chips were down, he was right there with his M-16. Doc liked to hang out with our squad. Sometimes he'd stay in one of our foxhole positions, and he would share guard. He was an all-around good guy and a competent medic.

Steve "Doc" Vincent in a bunker on guard duty, photo source Steve Vincent's family

On 13 February 1967, Operation Pershing began. We were air assaulted into the North Central Section of Binh Dinh Province near Highway 1. We had been told elements of the NVA 610th Division were active in this area, and our mission was to find and destroy them. We all knew the Tet truce was going to be a factor, so we had to be extra alert. There was no doubt the enemy had been resupplied and that we would see more action.

It was like a game of chase. We would make contact and kill a few of them, and then they would disappear. The danger of the chase is the enemy might be leading you into a trap. That's where Capt. Hitti excelled. He read the enemy well and used flanking maneuvers to heard the enemy into a position that was advantageous to us and for support from artillery and air power. We had many factors in our favor. The most important was to have leadership that knew how to use them to full advantage, and that's just what we had. The leaders we had were here to do a job and not for individual glory.

Our orders were to hold the line as the battalion shifted companies into blocking positions. C and D Companies had also made contact with the fleeing enemy. We learned we had lost six troopers in the firefight and had several wounded. Two of the casualties I personally knew. It was a very depressing thing to hear about these losses. It's another reminder of where we are and what we are doing. It's hard to comprehend the loss of someone. One day you see and talk to them, and maybe the next day, they are gone forever.

The open area was secured, and we received word that we would be setting up for the night. Positions were assigned, and we dug in. Our KIAs and wounded would be medevac'd from the clearing. Mike and I assisted with the bodies and loaded them on the Dustoff choppers. Mike knew all six troops, and he took it really hard. It is a grim assignment, but I always kept in mind that we were sending these guys home as quickly as possible. That's all we could do for them.

Mike and I joined Doc Vincent at our position and made more preparations for a long vigilant night. As darkness fell, artillery fire missions began outside our perimeter. When the shells exploded, some of the free-falling shrapnel was falling around us. If you got hit with a chunk of this, more than likely, you'd be cut and possibly burned because it was still red hot. Even though it posed some danger, it was very reassuring.

It was the 1st of March, and we were going to be making an air assault into the An Loa Valley. Everyone was as ready as they could be, but we had a foreboding as to what was ahead. The enemy had been much more aggressive since Tet, so we could only assume they had gotten the manpower and supplies that they so desperately needed.

A couple of hours into our second day, all hell broke loose in the distance. Small arms fire and grenades resounded across the valley. C Company had made heavy contact on the other side of the valley. Capt. Hatti was on the radio with the CO of C Company. He grabbed two platoons and started down the slope toward the valley below. We were instructed to continue in the same direction in case the enemy would try to flee in that direction.

I could hear all the communications over the radio as Capt. Hatti and 1st and 3rd platoons hurried to assist C Company. There were several casualties already. Our orders were changed. We were told to get down in the valley A.S.A.P. and prepare an

LZ for medivac choppers. We got down in the valley and moved across from where the 1st Platoon was located. We secured the area and made contact by radio with the medivac choppers that were now on their way. The small arms fire was still blazing up in the eastern massif, and we were taking sniper fire on the LZ.

We fired at will toward the muzzle flashes in the trees and for LT Foley's artillery fire mission at the western massif. The walking wounded from C Company began to appear on the LZ, and Doc Vincent and another medic ran to their aid. I could hear the whopping sound of approaching choppers. The gunships came in first and strafed the western tree line where the sniper fire was coming from. The medivacs came in, and one of our squads helped the wounded onto the choppers. We were securing the west side of the clearing. All firing had stopped on our side, and Lt Foley was pushing into the tree line with his platoon to see if there were any more snippers. He directed my squad to lend a hand with the evacuation of the dead and wounded.

There were many severely wounded, and they were the priority to evacuate. It was literally a bloody mess. I never got used to that sight. I had been in Nam for six months, and B Company had lost over 20 men and well over a hundred wounded. When considering the time and numerical strength of the company, that was a lot. All you had to do was look around, and there were many new faces. The company was turning over, and only a few of us were experienced troops.

Mike spotted Torres and me and came over and told us that Capt. Hatti had been wounded, and he saw him being evacuated. He said he didn't think his wounds were too bad because he walked to the chopper by himself. This was really bad news. Capt. Hatti was a really fine and capable officer and a true leader. We all knew that we would feel the loss of his leadership.

The night passed slowly, and there was no probing. The sun came up, and the whopping sound of helicopters awakened me. Torres and I grabbed our gear and headed to the LZ. We ran into Doc Vincent, and he told us where our platoon was and filled us in on what had taken place. Doc always had the inside scoop on what was going on. He was our best source of information because he was linked to the other medics and they exchanged info. He told us we were getting a new CO in a couple of days and that it wasn't Lt Grady. He told us he had talked to Capt. Hatti and that his wounds weren't life-threatening, and he expected to come back to the battalion after recovery.

The evening log ship came in with a nice hot meal, and also, our new CO Capt. Gibson. He was fresh from the states and had no combat experience. The Capt. called a company meeting after chow. He told us a little about himself and what he expected from us. It was a typical pep talk. Let's go get them and kick ass. I don't think he realized he was talking to troopers that had been doing just that for the last seven months.

We were standing in the rain waiting to be picked up by a chopper and air assaulted to Bong Son Plain. The mission would seek out elements of the 22nd NVA Division that were known to be in the area. Once again, this was supposed to be a large-scale operation, and to me, that was good news. It's like that old cliché, "there is safety in numbers."

Jim, a member of our troop, returned, and it was completely dark. He told us that Capt. Gibson was missing along with two of his RTOs. He was last seen advancing through an opening in the hedgerow. There were four KIAs and several wounded. He said that one of the new troops got scared and tossed a grenade over a nearby hedgerow and badly wounded three of our medics. One of the medics was Steve Vincent, our platoon medic and part of our little group. Steve would be a big loss to us and our morale. Jim didn't know how badly he was wounded, but past experience told us that he was gone for good.

It was another long and uncertain night. We had little knowledge of what was going on or what we were up against. We would just have to wait for daylight and hope for the best. Now with Doc Vincent wounded and gone, our main information link was gone.

Lt Sipple, acting platoon leader, sent two patrols out to see if they could locate Capt. Gibson and the RTOs. No more than a half hour went by, and one of the NCOs came and got six of us and told us to follow him with just our rifles. We crossed through the next hedgerow and about thirty more yards, and there were the bodies of Capt. Gibson and his RTOs. They had been killed by small arms fire, and they had been hit several times. It was apparent they died instantly.

We wrapped the bodies in ponchos and carried them back to our secure open area. We returned to our position to await further instructions from our squad leader, Randy. We were very quiet and really didn't say much to one another. It had been a very bad day for B Company. We had lost our company commander and six NCOs. There were eleven wounded, and three of them were medics, including our own, Steve Vincent. I had a sick feeling in my stomach and was having a hard time realizing these guys were gone.

Four of the six NCOs that were killed were experienced and original members of the battalion. Their loss would be greatly felt. Every firefight was causing us to lose more and more people. We were undermanned in almost every position, and the lack of experience was becoming a major problem. The company was now desperately in need of replacements.

The Dustoff choppers arrived, and we watched as the bodies of Capt. Gibson and the other fallen troops were being loaded for transport to LZ English and on to Saigon. A strange and empty feeling came over me as I watched the chopper lift off and back to the South as it climbed into the morning sky. The same thought that I had so many times before was on my mind again; one day, you are here, and in just a few moments, your life is ended. I couldn't help but wonder when it would be my time or if I would be lucky enough to make it out of this hell hole. As hard as I tried, I couldn't keep these thoughts out of my head.

We rejoined the company at a village near Duc Pho. I hooked up with my platoon, and Randy filled me in on our latest mission. When I looked around, there were a lot of new faces and names that I didn't know. B Company had lost thirty-four troopers and over one hundred seventy wounded. When you consider that Air Mobile company strength was one hundred twenty-five, you couldn't help but wonder if you're going to make it out of here in one piece. It was one of those stats that you tried not to dwell on, but as time went on, it became harder and harder not to.

Steve "Doc" Vincent, Jim Haggerty, and Rich Roderick

Photo from "1966 The Year of the Horse", written by Robert K Powers, source unknown

On 20 December 1966, Bob Wilbanks from WHO Radio Des Moines, Iowa, interviewed Steve "Doc" Vincent. Steve made the following comments during the interview.

When asked what is the difference between the Green-Line and being in the jungle? Steve replied, "The Green-Line is boring but a lot safer than being in the jungle near the VC." Then Mr. Wilbanks asked if Steve had any close calls while in the jungle. Steve replied, "I once had my canteen shot off me." Finally, Mr. Wilbanks asked Steve what he thought of the Vietnamese people.

Steve said, "I really feel bad for the women and children who've been impacted by the war."

Heroic as Hell- The Dustoff Pilots of the Vietnam War – Apr 22, 2019, Medevac Nam, by Nikola Budanovic, the Guest Author.

During those very risky moments, the medic and crew chief would jump into the fire and load casualties into the helicopter with the assistance of nearby soldiers.

Among a variety of iconic scenes of the Vietnam War depicted in movies, documentaries, and news coverage, there is one in particular that makes this "first-ever televised conflict" instantly recognizable. The image, accompanied by a specific sound, is the sight of a Bell UH-1 Iroquois or "Huey" flying over the jungle, suppressing enemy fire, deploying soldiers, or evacuating wounded GIs.

While helicopters were used to some extent in Korea, it wasn't until the Vietnam War that the idea of a helicopter ambulance corps was fully developed. This was due to the necessity of using aerial transport to evacuate the wounded in Vietnam, as dictated by the terrain. Since most of the combat activity was in the jungle, roads proved useless even if they were nearby.

Ambushes and mines made land routes very unpredictable, for the jungle belonged to the Viet Cong.

However, the skies were off-limits for the guerrilla forces, making the Huey one of the U.S. Army's most important assets.

The dedicated "Dustoff" men–the medics and pilots who rushed into "hot" zones and willingly risked their lives to rescue as many soldiers as they could. The name comes from the call sign of the 57th Medical Detachment, which began operating in Vietnam in 1962.

Dustoff in Nam, photographer unknown

"Dustoff" soon became synonymous with all helicopter ambulance units operating in Vietnam. A well-trained and experienced crew could provide medical treatment for wounded personnel in the field within just 35 minutes.

The crew usually consisted of four men—two pilots with one acting as a commander, a medic assigned to evacuate the wounded, and the crew chief whose role was also to keep the chopper in top condition. Once in action, the pilot and the helicopter commander remained in the aircraft, ready for take-off. The commander would maintain radio communication with the unit requesting evacuation and headquarters.

During those very risky moments, the medic and crew chief would jump into the fire and load casualties into the helicopter with the assistance of nearby soldiers.

It is important to note that most of these missions were undertaken during skirmishes, so the helicopter would often come under a rain of small arms and mortar fire from the enemy. Furthermore, the sheer size of a Huey would attract most of the enemy fire, making the evacuation crew an instant target.

The "Dustoff" men earned universal respect among Vietnam War servicemen due to their sacrifices and capabilities to act under such pressure.

Chapter 7: Christmas in Vietnam

20 Dec 66

Dear Grandma & Grandpa,

I decided it was high time I get a letter off to you. Got four of your letters here, and I haven't had time to answer one yet. I also got the funny paper and cigars. I sure enjoyed both.

We are starting to build our own barracks now, and should have it finished in four or five days. After the termites started eating everyone's gear, they decided they better get us off the ground. I had just finished building a wooden floor in my area too.

You wondered if some of the guys would get any mail or packages. We got enough packages now from different people in the states that every man in the battalion will have a package for Christmas. We all got a lot of fan mail. I'm getting so much mail over here the men handling it have to work day and night sorting it.

This new ink pen sure works well. I've written a lot of letters, and I won't miss a lick.

Well, I just got another one of your most welcome letters today, so I just got to get this finished, and in the mail, before the month is over, or next year, Ha!

You mentioned how people make a living. Well, some of them have land and cattle, so that's enough to feed them. They eat and work their cattle in the fields. They haul some of their crops to town and sell them. That old Papa San over where we were on that last mission was the Chief of the Village. He had land, cattle, and did laundry for the troops, so he was pretty well off. He was in charge of the food. He rationed it out to the rest of his people in his village.

Well, I washed a few clothes out by hand yesterday, down by the river. That little brush sure worked great and is just the right size. I use the big one too, to clean the mud off my shoes and brush the dirt off my wooden floor.

Really works well for that.

Well, I see Churdan kind of beat Lake City pretty bad the other night. That little town of Churdan must have a good team.

Well, the actors are over by Saigon. They are supposed to be here in a few days. It should be a pretty good show.

You mention the churches. We got some real outstanding churches in some of the battalions. A lot of these people in the Army are professional carpenters and bricklayers. Almost any job needs to be done, and you can find someone who'd do it.

Yes, I heard Connie was home. I wonder if she will stay or go back. That was funny about the big dog messing on Sparkie's porch. We sure have a lot of dogs about Sparkie's size over here, only they are a different color.

Well, here I am again. I will finish this letter tonight. I just got your letter with a calendar in it. That's just right, and the new pen does write on it. You don't have to send me a plastic one because I keep this one in my billfold.

I have plastic wrapped around it, so it won't get wet. I still got the one they gave to me at Ft Leonardwood, Missouri, and it's in fair shape.

Well, better bring this to a close. Thanks a million for the calendar, cigars, and newspaper. I like to read the funnies.

Leon

P.S. I had a man today interview me from Des Moines, Iowa, and he said it would be on the radio.

Christmas card to Leon's Grandparents from Leon

29 Dec 66

Dear Grandma and Grandpa,

I'll start this letter today and try to get it finished within five days received your newspapers and chewing tobacco a while back. So nice of you to send me things all the time. I'll stop by your pad one of these days and tell you how much I appreciate all you've done for me these past two years, for being Uncle Sam's boy.

You ask what type of chewing tobacco I like best. I get plug tobacco in 101 rations. So, I get plenty of that. I sure do like that beechnut. That last pack you sent me lasted just two days.

Say, sounds like those basketball girls are better than your ole boys' team. I always thought the boys were tops, but I don't know. That was a pretty good score 83-40 over Bayard.

Say you mention the parrots. Our parrot flew off about two weeks ago, and we haven't seen a sign of him since. He wasn't good for anything, anyway.

It's been raining every day off and on and this mud hole here is just like a hog waler. I got a fly mission to where our old mission was last. I got to pick up an RL 31. That's an axle and a roll of Comms wire. I leave at 7:00 in the morning, suppose to catch a plane at the airport, and it should be an exciting day.

I sure do like that raincoat Kermit sent me. I use it about every day. It sure saves me from getting wet.

I went and saw the Bob Hope show, and it rained about all the time it was on. I sure appreciated the raincoat then. That Bob Hope show sure was good.

We had a pretty good Christmas. The Red Cross gave presents to some Vietnamese kids. We had Christmas Day off, the first day off in five months.

You ask about how many are in our base camp now. Well, there are about 200 troops. You ask if there are *evergreen trees here. No, the only evergreen here is artificial. You ask if I've heard from Noseep. No, I haven't, and he's not much for writing letters anyhow, but I'll see him later.*

I don't know for sure where this next mission will take us, but wherever the most VCs are, that's where we'll go.

Well, here I am again, and I didn't go on the fly mission because I had to fish some wire lines that had to be in today, so don't know when I'll get away to go.

Well, those new boots I got just a few months ago are worn out already. So, I just walked over to supply and got myself a new pair. Sure is nice, when you don't have to buy anything. When I was on the last mission, I wore my boots 20 out of 24 hours a day. They sure get rough treatment, but so do my feet. I use medicated powder on them, that helps.

Here it is a day later, so decided to finish this letter today. I just got told an hour ago that I have to go out in the

field tomorrow. So, I got to start getting my gear ready to go. You never know how long you'll be out there. So, I guess I'll be leaving this nice soft bed for quite some time.

So, till I find time to write again, I'll close for now.

Leon

Comments from Interviewing Steve Streeter: Steve said, "I remember when the 12th Evac helped take wounded soldiers to see Bob Hope and a cast of celebrities when they came to Cu Chi. The show was amazing. They allowed us to take our patients close to the stage, and we saw Phyliss Diller, Anita Bryant, Joey Heatherton, Chris Noel, and others. We had a 72-hour truce with the Viet Cong, but as you can imagine, they didn't honor it. Bob Hope wasn't very happy when mortar shells started landing nearby, causing the show to end a little early."

Comments from Interviewing Steve Streeter: Steve said, "After the show, Phyliss Diller and Anita Bryant said they wanted to visit the 12th Evac to see the wounded patients that weren't able to make it to the show. Their appearance really picked up the patients' spirits, especially a young kid. Phyllis Diller went over to his bed, where he had nothing but a sheet over him. She just crawled right into bed with me. The soldier turned beet red, but he definitely had something to write home about in his next letter."

Joey Heatherton at Bob Hope Show, source unknown

Chapter 8: On the Green-Line - In A Company

From Army supporting documentation, the National Archives College Park, Maryland.

Camp Radcliff's perimeter is guarded by a "Green-Line." There are guard towers every fifty yards. To ensure a clear field of vision, they cleared foliage and added several rings of barbed concertina wire.

Additionally, they added booby traps and mines.

Each guard tower has three men and has to be manned 24 hours a day. For this, it takes most of a battalion of men to guard the camp perimeter. There's an M60 machine gun and a large searchlight. The towers are fifty feet high, which gives them a good field of vision. The platform is about six feet square. They are also sandbagged too, for additional protection from small arms fire.

Daily perimeter inspections are made to ensure everything is still secure, and nothing has been changed.

One individual could leave the tower during the day to allow time off. Periodically, battalion leadership will inspect the towers to ensure everything is operational and quiz guards with a series of questions to ensure they understand defensive procedures.

5 Jan 67

Dear Grandma and Grandpa,

I would have written you sooner, but I'm in one of those hard to get to places. They don't send our mail up here. The only way I can get it is to go down. I don't get down that often, so it's some time before I get to read your letters. I can send mail from here on the chow mule.

This tower I am at is about the highest tower around here, and it's straight up the hill about two miles. It's even hard for the mule to make it up here.

I received the flashlight today when I went down. It's just right. I didn't want it too big, because it would be hard to carry in my pocket. You are wondering what I use it for. Well, when I'm back at the main camp, I had to go out in the middle of the night repairing lines, and a flashlight helps to see, so I can make my splices. Then I use it to go to the outhouse at night, because no light in there, etc. Then up here on the Green-Line, I use it to dress with because no light here either. But when I go out where the VC is, it stays back in camp. We have Army flashlights, but there aren't enough for everybody, and most of the time they don't work. I have all kinds of batteries. Our section supplies batteries for all the other companies, so no problem there. Mom wrote me in a letter today that she sent me a flashlight too, so I'll have a spare in case one doesn't work.

I also received cigars and funny papers. I can make good use of both up here. Nothing to do but play solitaire and write letters, so you might be hearing from me more now. I also received your calendar and Dad sent me one too, so I can really start marking the days off.

You mentioned the picture Dad's got. Well, if I ever get where my buddy is and he's got his camera, I'll get one taken. That was when he got one of those new Polaroids, and he was trying it out on me.

You mentioned that steel helmet. I don't have to wear it around the main camp. But here on the Green-Line, I have to wear it on a mission.

Glad to see you have the old snake rattle. I was afraid you might throw it away.

I don't know if I mentioned it in my last letter, but I did see Bob Hope and he was really good.

Well, here I am again. This morning I had to go out in the open all day. I saw about a dozen monkeys out there swinging in the trees. Some of them are really big.

Well guess I better bring this to a close, I'll have to save something to write in my next letter.

Leon

Hon Cong Mountain Guard Tower overlooking Camp Ratcliff, source unknown

Comments from interviewing Frank "Hazel" Farrell: Frank said, "One time, I was heading to a guard tower to relieve one of the guys on shift. As I was climbing up the long ladder to the tower, one of the two guys in the tower shouted at me and said, "Look behind you," I turned around, and at the bottom of the steps was a black panther starting to climb the ladder. The guards distracted it as I flew up the ladder and dove into the tower."

7 Jan 67

Dear Grandma and Grandpa,

I bet you're surprised to hear from me again, so soon. I am bored with nothing to do, so decided to write you a few lines.

This Green-Line is about the most boring job I've ever had. It's even worse than pulling guard out on a mission. There is just nothing to do up here when it's my turn up in the tower. There are never more than three guys at the tower in the daytime, as the rest go on patrols.

I got out all my calendars and marked another day off. Got 197 days left over here.

It's really hard to write when I can't read your mail. I hope to get to go down next week and get my mail. I think I like it better up here than down in the main camp because down there I would be pulling KP, and I'll do anything to get out of that.

One thing is for sure, I got plenty of free time. We were supposed to be out on another mission by now, but I guess they aren't ready for us yet. I figure we will be out before the end of this month.

Well, how's your weather? Got down to 71 degrees here the other day, pretty cool.

Looks like I'm going to have to see the dentist again, before long. I got another tooth acting up. One thing is nice, you don't have to pay to get it done.

Well, I suppose everything is getting back to normal again after the holidays. It sure didn't seem like Christmas this year.

How is Lake City's basketball team doing by now? They should be in full swing now. How do you think they will do in the tournament? I haven't heard how Lander's team is doing, but they should place pretty well in the state.

Well, the old Papa Sans are quitting for the day. They usually stop at 3:30, then load them on trucks and take them to An Khe. The Papa Sans are kind of lazy, but the Moma Sans are good workers. They still got the old Papa Sans working on the fence. They are pretty slow, and of course, some of them look to be 80 years old. They get 75 cents a day. The interpreter gets $1.25 a day. They send these young kids to school to learn our language, then we tell them how we want the fence done, and they tell the old Papa Sans. The interpreter up here is about 13 or 14 years old.

Have you had any wild women get away lately? Do they still throw fits? Do you have many in the reformatory now?

Well, I guess I'll quit for now, didn't have much to say, but wanted to kill a little time. Been nice to visit. So long for now.

Leon.

12 Jan 67

Dear Grandma & Grandpa,

I got to go down to camp again the other day and pick up my mail. I got the funny paper, lemonade, and cigars, which I will use nicely in my long hours in the tower. Between that and my corn-cobb pipe, I try to keep occupied.

I think it is warming up some. It hasn't been as cold as before. This is the only place I know of where the sun shines when it's raining.

You mention the dogs. About a mile and a half from camp, we have a place where they keep these trained dogs. Must be about 50 of them. They all have dog houses and there's a company that takes care of them. I know you don't want to wander too close to them because they are trained to kill. They will take anybody unless you know their name or a word to control them.

I sure would like to have one of my own. I don't know if these other little dogs around here are rat terriers or not. Most of them are a little fatter than Sparkie. Most of them are tan in color.

You mentioned being tuned to that station of me on the radio. That could be a long time because the guy is still in Vietnam, and I think it won't be until he gets back. He never let me say much anyway because I told him how I hated the Army, I guess you are supposed to say you like the Army, but I told him just what I thought.

Sounds like Churdan must have an outstanding team. That was a pretty good score, so they must have made Churdan work for the victory.

Say you mention fish. I talked with these guys from the line companies I'm up here with. I'm with A company now, and one guy told me they were crossing the river, or rice paddy and a machine gun opened up on them. They had to go underwater and soak on the bottom. I guess it was about 8 ft deep. Anyway, when they got the machine gun nest knocked off, they came out of the water with fish in their pants, shirts, packs, and everywhere. I don't know what type of fish, but they got quite a few.

Well, I'm about to run out of things to say.

I want to thank you for the cigars and paper. I sure do appreciate you going to the trouble.

Tell Daryl I'm just burning up with so much energy. Wish I had some cows, and old pigs to feed night and morning.

That's about all I can think of. I think the old press is in bad shape for a weary hand. Got to make it last 194 days if possible. Glad I'm not in this place any longer than that.

Leon

Alpha Company crossing river in Bong Son, photo by Robert Matulac

On 20 December 1966, Bob Wilbanks from WHO Radio Des Moines, Iowa, interviewed Leon. The grandparents asked when his interview would be aired on the radio. Leon replied, "My interview might not make the cut because he didn't allow me to say too much. I was totally honest with him and told the guy what I thought. I said, "I hated the Army and didn't like being drafted into the Vietnam War."

Chapter 9: Scout Dogs Save Lives

From "The Dogs of the Vietnam War." Together we Served Blog.

Once in Vietnam, these dogs were the gold standard. Search-and-destroy missions used a handler and his scout dog to walk point out in the jungle, able to raise the alarm about an ambush long before most of the unit was in danger. The dog's handler could determine the distance to the danger, usually by the degree of his dog's state of "alert." Then, instead of walking into the Vietcong trap, he could call in fire or air support to obliterate the enemy position. Not every unit on patrol got a dog; there weren't enough to go around, and in those cases, a soldier would have to walk point alone. But with a scout dog team leading the way, most patrols were successful or uneventful.

A human nose has about five million scent receptors; a shepherd has at least 225 million. Dogs can detect movement much faster and more accurately than we can, and their ears can hear, even at a very early age, sounds from four times farther away than we can. What's more, all our dogs had lived with our American "smells" for years. The scent of the Vietnamese was very different and much easier for them to pick up and alert on.

Between the years 1964 through 1973, America deployed an estimated 4,000 war dogs and 10,000 handlers to help defend South Vietnam from invasion by North Vietnam. During the ground war, Veterinarians and Vet Techs were also deployed throughout South Vietnam to help manage the diets and medical health of war dogs.

The success of the war dogs and handlers in walking point, tracking, guarding, patrolling, and protecting American lives and military assets, ultimately reduced the enemy's capacity for surprise attacks. As a result, the enemy placed a price tag on the heads of the war dog teams and hunted them with extreme prejudice.

Scout dog and handler, photo by Robert Matulac

Vietnam War Dogs, November 9, 2013, by Fred Childs, from Vietnam War Dogs1965-1972; https//charliecompany.org/charlie-company/troops.

The decision to classify the war dogs as equipment and leave them all behind (several thousand) after the war remains the saddest chapter in America's military working dog history. Their final fate was either to be transferred to the South Vietnam Army or to be euthanized after each war dog unit was methodically and strategically deactivated throughout South Vietnam. Very few dogs were redeployed to U.S. bases outside of South Vietnam to live out their lives in peace. And there was no war dog adoption law until the year 2000 when WWII Marine War Dog Platoon Leader/Veterinarian Dr. William Putney made it happen with the help of U.S. Congressman Roscoe Bartlett of Maryland.

The German shepherd dog was the only breed trained for this job. The handler and dog led combat patrols and provided an early silent warning of danger. A scout dog team was deployed as "point man," which is the most vulnerable and dangerous position of a tactical formation moving through enemy territory. Scout dogs were trained to alert on enemy movement, booby traps, land mines, base camps, underground tunnel complexes, and underground caches of weapons, food, and medical supplies. The U.S. Army had the highest number of infantry scout dog teams deployed throughout South Vietnam and consequently suffered the highest number of casualties, dogs and handlers, of the war.

1973 is significant because that was when the United States ceased ground combat operations and withdrew the last of its ground combat forces from South Vietnam. The several thousand surviving war dogs were crated and no longer performing their jobs in the field because their masters were ordered out of South Vietnam. South Vietnam fell to North Vietnam in 1975, which officially ended the war.

Dog Becomes a Fighter When the Pressure's On Pacific Stars and Stripes, July 22, 1967, p7, Tokyo, Tokyo, JP, https//newspaperarchive.com/pa-stars-and-jul22-1967-p-7

BONG SON, Vietnam (10)— "I'd rather been shot than that dog. She saved my life twice that day," said Staff Sgt. Harry Coit of the 1st Air Cav. Div.'s 5th Bn., 7th Cav. Coit had doubts about the scout dog named Krim, who was working with his platoon during Operation Pershing. He claimed it lacked drive and had passed several booby traps without giving an alert. Coit was even thinking of having the dog sent back for further training.

Spec. 4 Michael Lister, the dog's handler, and Krim showed their value and left no doubt in Coit's mind that they were a valuable team. A Co. was moving cautiously along a trail deep in the jungle 250 miles north of Saigon when Krim gave her first alert. Upon investigation, the troopers found fresh enemy positions. In the next 30 minutes, the dog and handler alerted the infantrymen eight more times. Then Krim gave two strong alerts, and Lister pointed them out. Just then, the enemy opened fire from one position and hurled a grenade from the other. Lister saw the grenade coming through the air. He killed one enemy soldier. The rest withdrew.

After evacuating a wounded squad leader, A Co. went in pursuit. They chased the enemy for about an hour, and then Krim gave another strong alert but, this time did not wait for her handler to inform the infantrymen. She jumped into a bush where three enemy soldiers were waiting in an ambush and fought the enemy until one shot her. Medic Pfc. Gerald K. Robinson came up and gave the dog first aid. Krim had been shot through the nose but calmly let Robinson administer to her wounds. Men of the company improvised a stretcher for the dog and gave her water out of their canteens. They knew that a lot of them were still alive because of the dog's alertness and courage.

Later, the men of the company sent a letter of thanks to 'Mrs. Betty Rowe, of Midland. Mich., who donated Krim. Lister of San Antonio, Texas, and Krim were both put in for a Bronze Star with a "V" device for valor in combat.

18 Jan 67

Dear Grandma and Grandpa,

I got to go down a few days ago and pick up my mail, so I have a few letters to answer. I sure was glad to receive your most welcome letters. I sure do look forward to each and every one.

I made a New Year resolution. I forgot to tell you about it in my last letter. I went to the dentist to make an appointment to get some teeth filled. He couldn't get to it before my mission so he told me I better lay off the tobacco and brush my teeth pretty often till he can work on them. So, I just quit altogether.

Say, that Holstein steer sure was ripe. I bet it took a lot of groceries to make him tip the scales that heavy. We have an old brown Swiss steer that's been at the county fair for the last 7-8 years that's about that same size. He's so fat he can hardly get up and down by himself. Logan packing owns him. Poor old fella has it tough when it's hot.

Well, last night they brought out two half gallons of ice cream for five of us, that was all of us here at the time. So, me and ole Bacon ate ½ gallon ourselves. We were cold but we ate it anyway. It sure was good. That's one thing you don't get over here very often.

If you heard it was getting pretty hot over here, it must be someplace else. Because I wear a wool sweater shirt and jacket all day long, and I sure don't sweat at all.

You ask about my weight. Well, I can't see that I'm gaining or losing any weight.

You ask how big the cattle are over here. Well, they are pretty small. Don't get over 400 lbs at the most. The average is around 225# to 250#. Those water buffalo are big. They must weigh nearly a ton. These cattle I think belong to a whole village when you see 20 or 30 in one bunch. Then you see a guy with two or three leading them to a place to graze alongside rice paddies, or anywhere they can find a little grass. When they are moving from one place to another, they have a little bamboo basket they slip over their heads so they won't eat on the way to the pasture. Most of them are broke to lead.

I don't hear from Noseep, but I'm pretty sure he's still in Japan.

Say this would be a good climate over here for Sparkie because it's only cool about two months out of 12. December and January are the coldest months over here in some places that are, and I'm in one of those places.

Grandma, that was quite a write-up about those old gals trying to get away, so I guess you had some excitement around there.

This place I'm on the Green-Line, and it's about five miles from base camp. I sleep in a ratty old hut with sandbags for a floor. It does keep the wind out pretty good, and the rats only chew on me at night. I sleep with my boots on, so they won't chew on my toes.

I didn't go on that trip to get RL-31, because I had to go to the field instead.

Sounds like Mom and Dad had plenty of help to move. I hope this will be their last. That should be a good place for the Men, town is a poor place for kids their age to grow up.

Well, can't think of much more to say. My next letter should have a little better news because I should be heading out on the mission. The old press still runs pretty well, I guess after all. Will close now.

Leon

Comments from interviewing Frank "Hazel" Farrell: Frank said, "You always had to watch for snakes and rats. The rats were bad at night, and you could see them running across the opening to our bunker. Several guys got bit and had to have shots in their stomachs for rabies. Needless to say, we all slept with our boots on."

Vietnamese girl helping her Papa San with cattle, source Steve Vincent

24 Jan 67

Dear Grandma and Grandpa,

I received your most welcome letters, newspapers, and tobacco today, so will try and write a few lines and thank you for the tobacco, although I said I quit chewing. I guess it wouldn't hurt to sneak a chew in now and then.

I am supposed to be leaving the Green-Line tomorrow. You say you don't know what I mean by Green-Line.

Well, it's a string of lights and towers all the way around Ratcliff, that's the name of the camp here. These towers are about 50 yards apart for

many miles. The lights are on cement poles that are about 25 feet apart. They call this the Green-Line. Green means safe and red means danger. Then at night, we have 10-12 guys up here to pull guard on the tower.

The OP and LP haven't been going out lately, so we only have been pulling about three hours during the daytime, and we are off until night. OP means a forward observation post which is about 2000 meters to our front. They just go out there and monitor the radio all night, and in the morning if there had been any action that night. They go out on LP, long-range patrol scouting the area for VC. Then they send this LP out during the daytime. Only a different bunch of guys to scout areas, and look for signs of VC. I'll only be with A Company for a few more days, then I'll go back to headquarters.

You ask how far we are from base camp. It's about 5 miles straight down. We are right in front of the old Hon Cong Mountain. Then we watch for VC from the tower with all kinds of weapons in it. We have an M-79 grenade launcher that will completely blow up a building.

You mention an outhouse in our tower. This tower isn't that big. It's about 5 by 5 all the way around. At the top, it stands about 30 feet in the air.

You mention picking up my mail. I have to go to my company area, which is about 5 miles from here.

I work with about 10 to 12 guys up here around the tower. Then behind it, there is a big searchlight, and a generator to run it. The engineers have a big bunker built near it, and they operate the light. I sleep on the ground with a sandbag wall and a canvas roof.

Haven't seen Steve V. for a long time now. I don't see much of anybody out here; except the guys, I work with. Ole Nicks is down on Tower 5 and I'm on 6. I see him once and a while.

We haven't seen any VC around here, but at night they pick them up on the radar and shoot mortars at them, and AR automatic rifles from choppers. None of my old buddies are up here, but I got new ones now, after being around a person for 30 days you get to be pretty good buddies.

Sure glad to hear Daryl got a new loader. I'll have to go visit him now and see how it works. Sounds like cattle prices are fair. I'd sure like to see Harley's sale. He's got some good calves.

Well like they say, summer is just starting here. Starting to warm up a lot this last week. Guess I've said enough, for now, so will close till next time.

Leon

Comments from interviewing Frank "Hazel" Farrell: Frank said, "Patrols were very dangerous, especially when you had to go into villages looking in each hooch for enemy caches. We had to be extra careful, and it was so difficult to determine who was friendly and who was VC because they all looked alike. One day they could be friendly villagers, and the next, VC. Even the children were potentially dangerous and could come up to you begging for food and toss a grenade in your lap. Frank added, I would go into a hut and had to be extra careful because of booby traps. I remember raising the bed and finding US rifles, ammunition, and supplies, which had been collected by the VC."

28 Jan 67

Dear Grandma & Grandpa,

Well, I went down to base camp just a few days ago, so got a chance to pick up my mail. Glad to receive your package of cigars, lemonade, and your welcome letter.

It's sure starting to get hot here again so lemonade tastes really good when a person's hot and dry.

I saw Steve V. a little while when I was down at the camp. He just got back from 14 days of RR. That's rest and relaxation. They give a person a chance to go to some country over here, just to relax for a while. I am supposed to go in March if I go. I don't much care if I go or not.

Say you wanted a picture of me, well this one you probably can carry in your billfold, and it's a picture of me. Byrd took this picture of me when I was putting telephone lines into a cable to run to the switchboard, which is inside the steel building in the corner. Swamp Rat was up on the pole-tying line. Tell me, does it look like I've changed any?

I'm still here on the Green-Line and was supposed to go on a mission today, but don't have anybody to relieve us on the Green-Line, etc. Might not go till the 15th of February now.

Don't worry about my teeth. I have an appointment at this surgical medicine to get them all fixed on the 3rd of February.

You ask about the Vietnamese workers that are building the fence. The Army doesn't feed them, they bring their rice with them. They are all done with the fence now. They got them on the road shoveling ditches and moving rocks.

I don't do much wire laying here now. If one happens to break near the towers, I have to fix it, but Nick takes care of most of that. Back at base camp they really been laying cement, and building barracks. I sure got an easy job compared to those poor boys back there. I don't even pull that darn old KP, one thing I hate worst of all. I would pour cement a month before I would mess with those pots and pans.

This place our tower is on is big enough to turn a 2 ½-ton truck around with little work, but it isn't big.

Say I'm doing all right for an old press, that didn't have much to write about when I started.

Well, as you notice in my picture, no spit-shined boots, or pressed uniform. Don't even have my stripes on, so they aren't too strict on how a person looks.

Got a letter from the Allens, guess they wish I was there to drive the old team. They are getting ready to calve next month.

Well, guess I better bring this to a close. Thank you for the newspaper, and things.

Leon

Leon Toyne pulling telephone lines for a switchboard,
photo source Leon Toyne family

1 Feb 67

Dear Grandma & Grandpa,

I received your most welcome letter, cigars, and funny papers today. I had so much mail the old sergeant brought it up to me. So, when I'm on guard I blow some on the bugs and spit tobacco on the rats at the bottom of the tower.

How do you like this paper and the green ink pen Chaplin gave me? He comes up and gives us a sermon every Saturday afternoon. We have it Saturday because he's really busy on Sunday. He's just a pretty nice guy.

I am still up here on the tower, looked to be going out on an operation anytime now. It's been just pretty warm this last week.

Sounds like you are having quite a few cattle being sold here lately. Sounds like Harley did all right on his calves. When I saw his calves last summer, they looked pretty good to me.

Sounds like Lake City's basketball team isn't doing too hot. How many games have they won this season so far? I think Lander's team will place 2nd or 3rd in the state. They are just a pretty good team this year.

Well, I don't have anything very interesting to tell you. Don't do a thing but pull my guard in the tower, chew tobacco, and spit on the rats. This shouldn't last too much longer. I'm surprised we're still here, we were supposed to leave here 4 or 5 days ago, and I don't much care if I leave here or not. I'm kind of beginning to like it up here. I sure do keep them rats running and have a lot of time to write letters.

Got a letter from Billy T., he's got the same problem. He just drives the Post bus to Memphis and has nothing to do the rest of the time. I figure they will put me to work before too long, so I shouldn't gripe at this little rest.

Thanks for everything.

Leon

Comments from interviewing Frank "Hazel" Farrell: Frank said, "One of the duties I was called upon to do was a guard or protect the Chaplin since he didn't carry a weapon. He visited the troops in the field and traveled by jeep to various LZs and firebases." Frank added, "The Chaplin would go to the field regularly to provide spiritual support and sermons to the troops."

Chapter 10: LZ English – LZ Hump

6 Feb 67

Dear Grandma & Grandpa,

I received your most welcome letters and cigars along with newspapers. That sure was a big windstorm they had.

I guess I should tell you not to send any more cigars, although I sure do enjoy them. They are broken up so bad

that it's hard to salvage even one good one, I guess I don't need them anyway. They keep me so busy I don't have time to smoke anyhow.

I am 160 miles from base camp. I flew here by airplane. This LZ we are at is LZ English, and it's sure back in the jungle. I've been digging a bunker, putting in lights, and telephone lines, and operating a switchboard at night. Now we are cutting bamboo back in the jungle and using it for telephone poles. We have to have them in the air because we have a cat clearing the area for our tents and making roads.

There's no PX, no showers, so it's going to be a long dirty old 4 months. It sure is hot and I've really been using a lot of sunscreen. My nose is one big blister.

I gave up on my teeth for a while. I have to fix them later. They aren't hurting anyway. They keep me going 24 hours a day. So, when I get a chance to sleep, I sure take it. There won't be any guard-pulling duty for me this time. They still give you a lot of ice cream and it sure is good in the hot weather, and I never get a belly ache.

Well, so it's 1:00 in the morning, so maybe I can finish this letter if the switchboard will stop ringing long enough. Sure is a lot of action in this new area. I'm just two miles from Bong Son and the people sure aren't very friendly, so there will be no Papa San this time. I sure don't like this area, but I guess over here you don't get what you like.

I'm kind of glad I'm not pulling guard this time because it looks to be a pretty dangerous job here. There's VC in this area so I'm sure we will be here for 4 months, if so, this will be the last dangerous operation.

Well, there's no more I can think of to write, so will close for now. I don't know how often I'll get to write, so don't be surprised if you don't hear from me too often.

Leon

P.S. I also got the package with the gum in it. I still chew a lot of gum, thank you.

McGarrigle, George L. (1998). Taking the Offensive: October 1966 to October 1967. Center of Military History, United States Army.

During the last two weeks of January, the ARVN fought two major battles against the 7th and 8th Battalions of the 22nd Regiment and, with timely American assistance, claimed to have killed or captured over 250 PAVN. Then, on 2 February, Norton (Maj Gen Norton, Commander 1st Cavalry Division) received an urgent report indicating that two PAVN battalions would attack Pony, an American firebase in the northern Kim Son Valley, sometime during the next seven days. Given what happened at Bird in the same general area, Norton reacted quickly and airlifted the 3rd Brigade headquarters with one battalion from Camp Radcliff to Pony.

Another intelligence source, a defector from the 9th Battalion, 22nd Regiment, revealed that his unit was understrength but had plenty of ammunition and was planning to attack LZ English after the TET truce between 8 and 12 February. Norton strengthened the base's defenses and deployed additional 2nd Brigade units around it. The third piece of information, provided by US signal intelligence, pinpointed the command post of the PAVN 3rd Division in the An Lao Valley. Capturing such an important target would be a significant coup, and Norton sent an entire battalion to locate and destroy it. Although unable to find the actual headquarters, the American force came upon a major PAVN supply base containing several tons of food and supplies. On 6 February, the ARVN 40th

Regiment, 22nd Division, met a PAVN battalion 4 km north of English and routed it in a short, violent fight. Accompanying US advisers reported counting over 100 PAVN dead.

11 Feb 67

Dear Grandma & Grandpa,

Well, it's 3:00 in the morning, and I got a lot of free time, so decided to write you a few lines, and thank you for the package. These guys around here think I got pretty nice grandparents, to send me packages and mail all the time.

I've been really busy up here for the last day or two. We got most all our lines in now, and a pretty good bunker, so there isn't a real lot left to do. We are still building a few bunkers, etc. We are still trying to get most of our tents down, so everyone will be on the ground in a bunker. Charlie hit us with mortars two nights ago, so we find it's best to be in a deep hole with strong walls because old Charlie is pretty active around here.

You ask where we hang the wire. Well in base camp, most of it hangs from telephone poles, some from trees. Out here we've been cutting bamboo to hang our lines on, but a lot of it lies on the ground. A lot of times in the middle of the night we have to lay an emergency line so we don't take time to put it in the air, so we just have it on the ground.

I don't know if I told you in my last letter, that we have a little gray monkey in the platoon. We feed him about anything they caught out in the jungle. We only had him here for two days and took him forward to LZ Hump. He belongs to the radio section.

Sounds like you are still having pretty cool weather back there. So hot here that it's hard to sleep at night. Well, 170 days left, that's about all I can think of for now.

Leon

P.S. Thanks a million for the package.

LZ Hump Chinook with Howitzer, photo from the National Archives, College Park, Maryland

14 Feb 67

Dear Grandma & Grandpa,

Well so here I am again, so will try to get off a few lines this morning.

I received your most welcome package a few days ago. With cigars, chewing tobacco, candy, and also gum. So, while I'm on the switchboard I spit, blow smoke, and chew. By the time I get done my three hours are pretty much over.

I don't do hardly anything, but I sure don't get very much sleep. We usually have to get up in the middle of the night and put in an emergency wire line to some big wheel. Can't use a flashlight because of afraid the VC will spot you, so it gets pretty hard stumbling around in the dark trying to get a line in. Then we are always finding something to do in the day. Putting lines in the air or fixing areas.

Did I tell you we have a hot plate right by the switchboard and a cupboard with food in it? So, we drink coffee and eat all the time. I'm beginning to like coffee now. It helps me keep awake during those wee hours of the morning.

I need to tell you about a site that's something real pretty that I've seen twice since I've been here. They're flying a lot of other outfits in here besides the 7th Cav. Because of so many Charlies. One evening about an hour or less before dark we had an air strike. 20 helicopters came here, landed, and hit the air all at once; sure would have been a pretty sight if I would have had a *camera. Then they kept landing here, dropping VC prisoners off. Wow this place was like the main street in Denver only all the traffic was in the air.*

Well, guess I better bring this to a close.

Sorry, you know that a black marking pen doesn't work too well to write letters. Old Swamp Rat gave me that because he had bought so many, from the Vietnamese locals.

Guess I will shut the press down now.

Leon

P.S. 167 days till <u>FREEDOM.</u>

17 Feb 67

Dear Grandma & Grandpa,

I received your most welcome letter today, and funny papers, with cigars. So will see if I can find a few lines to write.

Well, it's about the same here although we see a lot of action. Still building a few bunkers. The weather here has been pretty warm, but not real hot. I run around without a shirt a lot of the time.

Say old Carroll beat Lake City pretty bad didn't they, 124-50 is quite a score.

You mention me sleeping in my clothes, well I do. A lot of guys wear their clothes for around 45 days before they rot off. I usually wash mine out by hand before I let them rot off. If a person tears a hole in them, you just walk over to supply and take the holey ones off and put on a new set, and wear them till they rot off.

You ask about Sharon, she's a special friend from Crowheart, Wyoming. A horse is nice, but you can't take them everywhere, and some gals, they sure are poor cooks. I guess I better watch what I write if these letters are making the rounds.

Well, every morning for the past week I've been going to the dentist here out in the field. About two more trips and I should be done for a while. This also helps to keep me out of KP, because I have an appointment every morning, but that won't work forever. Pretty soon I'll run out of teeth to fill. Frank Farrell, nickname "Hazel", had KP today, so suppose I'll be next before long. Just 164 days left so that makes me feel pretty good.

I sure have a lot of free time on my hands when I'm operating this switchboard. During the days there are always lines to fix, and a lot of times at night we have to go fix them. Yes, today we had three go out. Seems like somebody is always driving over them and hooking machinery on them, breaking them. Then we have to be careful about putting them in the air, because of so many choppers. There must be close to 100, right in this small area, we are set up.

Well, there's not much more I can think of, for now, so guess I better close.

I want to thank you for the things you sent me. Looks like I have no further traffic at the time for your station, so here's me saying "roger out".

164 <u>DAYS</u> Leon

25 Feb 67

Dear Grandma & Grandpa,

I received your most welcome letter, a package of gum, and Kool-Aid a few days ago. I also got a note from a couple of little girl cousins, kind of nice.

Well, here it is at 12:30 after midnight, and I'm operating the switchboard, and all I got is time. So, I will see if I can make some kind of letter out of this mess. I'm also sipping on some hot cocoa while I write. There are also all kinds of chow to eat if I get hungry during the night. Well enough for the daily report, now get down to a little transmitting here.

I suppose it's still a little cool in the flat country. Well, out here in the middle of nowhere, it's just plain hot, so hot it's hard to sleep at night.

Grandpa, it sure sounds to me like your girls had a bad year this year for the basketball side of it. Well, maybe better luck next season.

This place around here looks like a prairie dog town. There's hardly a tent up. Everybody is living under the ground. We are deep enough so a person can stand up straight and walk around without banging his head on the roof.

Yesterday my big toe came sticking right through a hole in my sock, so I just walk over to supply, took off my boot, and showed him my toe, and he gave me two new pairs of socks. So, whenever you have holes, no problem with sewing it. You just tell the man and he will give you a new one.

No rats to spit on around here, so I don't chew very much tobacco now.

The other day Harry brought his monkey over for us to keep. He would eat and drink out of a glass just like a person. We had a little dog around here too, and the monkey was always jumping on the dog's back for a full ride somewhere.

Well, guess I better close for now.

<u>151 DAYS</u> Leon

3 Mar 67

Dear Grandma & Grandpa,

I received another package with Kool-Aid, gum, and a funny paper in it today. I got three letters since I wrote

you, so decided I better write you a few lines to let you know what's happening. I've sure been doing good about receiving my mail. I got twelve letters in two days. Wow!

It sure was hot here. I got a blister on my lip and it sure hurts. I've been using a lot of Chapstick on it, and it seems to help, but sure hurts. I'll have to see if I can get out some chewing tobacco, and see if that will help make it worse.

We get 101 rations every day now, so I get plenty of cigars now, which makes me happy along with the tobacco. I think there are only two of us in the whole battalion that chews. Seems like everybody always wants to give me a plug. They all know I like to chew it. We also got soap, toothpaste, razor blades, candy, etc.

I do like that Kool-Aid you send because it's sure good when it's so hot. I also chew a lot of gum to clean my jaw after I get rid of my cud. It gives a good taste and keeps a person from getting so thirsty.

Well, I've still been doing a little work on my bunker, got it looking just pretty nice.

The past night I really worked hard for a few hours, as we had one of those main lines go out just before dark. I didn't want to go out there alone because it was a long way, and not real safe. So, I got myself a jeep and a driver and I worked about 3 hours on it. The road traffic had worn it out in about 6 places and it was pitch dark. I didn't dare use a light, so it was a tough job finding the breaks in the dark. The CO put out a work order if a person went out at night, he had to have a person ride shotgun. I sure was glad of that.

I sure don't get much sleep in the middle of the night, a lot of fixing lines. We have 30 to take care of now, and it sure keeps a person going. I try to get 5 hours of sleep every night, if possible, sometimes I get six, but I haven't for a long time.

This switchboard takes a lot of a person's spare time because it has to be run 24 hours a day, and we only got three operators. Plus, we have the 30 lines, and also lights. It's not really hard to work, but for the long hours, a person puts in.

You ask what LZ English is, well that's the name of our location where we are set up now. There are landing zones set up all over. There's one on the other side of ours named LZ Dog. LZ is where the headquarters part of the battalions operates from when we have wire lines running to these different outfits set up out here. The longest line we have to fix is about 3 miles. We have communications clear back to An Khe which is 160 miles from here.

You mentioned writing by candlelight, that's a negative on that. We have two 60w bulbs in our bunker. That candle wax was from roasting marshmallows. We have big generators that supply our light electricity. We have to plug all the holes so no light gets out at night, so Charlie can't snipe at us.

This LZ we are in is not going to be a permanent camp. All we build is sandbag bunkers and then we will go off and leave them when it's time to go.

You ask what I sleep on. An air mattress on top of steel stakes laying across bags. That's the number one bed around here, any time you have an air mattress.

That monkey you mention is about the size of a big rat. Nick has him out at his bunker. Now we all pass him around and share him. He is fun to hang around with.

We have our own mess hall here, so we don't have food flown into us. The line crews out in the jungle have there's flown into them. As near as I know this place is about 75 miles from where we were at for our last operation.

Well, it's about 3:00 in the morning, time for me to go get some shut-eye, so will bring this to a close. Got a minute, so will say some more. Thank you for the package. Happy Birthday, Grandma, a little late, but I remembered.

I had an accident last night, which I forgot to tell you about. Bent over and ripped a big hole in my britches. So went over to supply, took them off, and got a new pair, sure handy. I don't know if they ripped from being worn for 40 days or just plain getting fat.

<u>150 DAYS</u> Leon

Comments from interviewing Frank "Hazel" Farrell: Frank said, once and a while, our radio would go out in the middle of the night due to the comm line being cut or broken by jeep or truck traffic. So, we had to go out in the jungle in the middle of the night and weld it back together. We couldn't use light because of the VC, so we had to feel our way around." Frank added, sometimes we would go 2-3 days with little or no sleep."

Jerry Nicholson (Nick) and Frank Farrell (Hazel) with "Joe" the monkey at LZ English, photo source Frank Farrell

7 Mar 67

Dear Grandma & Grandpa,

Wow! I sure am tough. I've been up all night except for 1 ½ hours' sleep. Wow! I'm sure tough and that isn't all. I got a sore lip that hurts like hell! Tough enough though, and I live like a prairie dog and can sleep standing up. I can take it because I come from a good bloodline. I was built to be tuff. Is that the way you spell tuff or is it this tough, any way you know what I mean don't you? Don't get the idea I'm going crazy. Got to be tough to put up with these hammer-headed sergeants. You run into a jughead, hammer-headed, knock-kneed, overbearing, swivel-hip horse once in a while. They can be corrected in some cases, but some of these sergeants are just plain worthless.

So old Sparkie is kind of fussy about what he eats. I wonder how Sparkie would like to latch on to a monkey's tail. Joe, the monkey was playing in front of our hutch. This pup came along and bit into Joe's tail and old Joe jumped all over the pup. He was on his back pulling at the pup's ears and chattering at him. If a person ever pinches a monkey or teases him, he gets mean. The monkey eats mostly bread and eggs, that's what he likes best, but he'll eat anything.

Hey Grandma, don't worry about boring letters. I like them any way I can get them. You mention Sharon, she's real nice, she and I are "heart with an arrow threw It". But I have four other girls that write also. So never do mention them to her, might not think it's a joke.

Grandma, don't worry about my teeth. I already had $150 worth filled. Remember I'm tough and it doesn't bother me. "Pain!"

So, your old girls still try to break out. They must be pretty wild old gals. A person always looks for a gal with a little spunk anyway, Ha!

Grandpa, Churdan went to the tournament, huh? I thought they would, by the scores you wrote about. Say, I got them funny books, real nice. Already read all three.

Grandpa, if you got a toothache, put a good chew of tobacco on it, won't ache anymore.

Leon

Chapter 11: LZ Pony - LZ Sandra

12 Mar 67

Dear Grandma & Grandpa,

I received your most welcome letter a few days ago, so will try and drop you a few lines. I was also real happy to get the funny papers and gum.

Well, I moved to a new location, since I wrote you last. I went by Charlie to LZ Pony. They needed a switchboard and two operators to handle the shotgun and the 2-3 shop telephone calls. The shotgun is a big shot switch that's where all the brains hand out information from our 2-3. It keeps track of our line companies and their contact with Charlie. A Charlie, Charlie is a chopper.

Hazel, a radio telephone operator (RTO), and I are the only ones operating this switchboard out here at LZ Pony. Sure are some long hours, as we have to operate it 24 hours a day. We pull 4 hours on and 4 hours off.

Frank Farrell "Hazel" and Leon Toyne at LZ Pony, photo source Frank Farrell

This LZ Pony isn't much of a place. Pretty secure, but it's in the middle of nowhere. It's kind of a little hole with mountains all around it. Back at LZ English, Nick had to take over my job running the main switchboard.

I also received some good news here the other day. They had me fill out a slip asking me if I want to extend over here or get out early. So, I will be out of Vietnam by August 1st and be discharged in Oakland by the 15th of August. It sure made me feel good.

You ask about Steve V. I saw him once from a distance, but never got to talk with him. I probably won't see him out here at LZ Pony. He stays in the field most of the time.

Grandpa, sure sorry to hear you had so much trouble with your teeth. I know how it feels. If I ever get my lip healed up, I have to go back and get some more done on mine. My lip sure has been giving me trouble. It must be the climate causing some of the trouble. I told them it was contagious, so I won't be able to pull KP, but it really isn't that bad. There's no KP out here at LZ Pony anyway. Our chow comes by chopper.

Say you mention that monkey. That Monkey sure likes Nick. It gets a little cool sometimes at night, so Joe the monkey climbs inside Nick's shirt and curls up, and goes to sleep. Nick's taking care of Joe now. If you come near Joe, he will start unbuttoning your pockets and starts taking things out. Seems like Joe's always climbing all over a person.

If this letter seems to be going downhill, it's because I am so sleepy, I can hardly keep my eyes open, so now you see why I have to be so tough. Well, I get off at 1:00 AM, which is about 30 minutes away and then I go back on at 5:00 AM.

Well, I guess I will bring this to a close.

<u>141 DAYS</u> Leon

Photo of a helicopter landing at LZ Pony, obtained from National Archives, College Park, Maryland

A Radio Operator (RTO) hazardous Duty in Vietnam

Shortly after 11 a.m. on July 1, 1970, Capt. Bill Williams, commander of Bravo Company, 2nd Battalion, 506th Infantry Regiment, 101st Airborne Division, and two radiotelephone operators with AN/PRC-25 radios jumped from their Huey helicopter. They immediately drew fire. The North Vietnamese Army placed a high priority on destroying the radios or killing their RTOs. THE 'MOST IMPORTANT TACTICAL FIELD ITEM' IN THE VIETNAM WAR WASN'T A WEAPON By CARL O. SCHUSTER 2/24/2022

"The Most Important Tactical Field Item" in the Vietnam War | History Net.

RTO and his Commander await the second wave of Combat helicopters at isolated LZ for Operation Pershing photo from National Archives, College Park, Maryland,

Developed in the late 1950s as a replacement for the Korean War-era AN/PRC-10, the AN/PRC-25, or "Prick 25," incorporated pioneering solid-state circuitry. Additionally, it was water resistant, simple to operate, and easy to maintain. Its 50 Hz "squelch feature," muting routine background noise when a strong signal wasn't detected, simplified tuning.

The radio had two antennas, a 3-foot standard antenna for most missions and a 10-foot long-range antenna carried in a canvas bag attached to the radio's side. U.S. Special Forces and long-range reconnaissance patrols developed improvised "jungle antennas" that extended the range even farther.

The AN/PRC-25 pack consisted of two metal cans. The lower can contained the battery pack; the upper the transceiver. The radio proved to be almost "soldier-proof" in the field. The handset was vulnerable to moisture.

Most RTOs pulled the battery pack's clear plastic wrapping over the handset, securing it with a rubber band. The batteries were good for two to three hours of heavy use and could last for several days if used sparingly. The radios also could run off a vehicle's power supply. The battery packs had to be destroyed when expended since the NVA used them in booby traps.

The "Prick 25" entered Vietnam in 1965 and was carried on virtually all land vehicles, riverine craft, and aircraft. Gen. Creighton Abrams, deputy commander and then commander of Military Assistance Command, Vietnam, called the Prick 25 "the single most important tactical field item in Vietnam." Adopted by more than 30 U.S. allies, the AN/PRC-25 remained in service well into the 1980s.

U.S. allies, the AN/PRC-25, remained in service well into the 1980s.

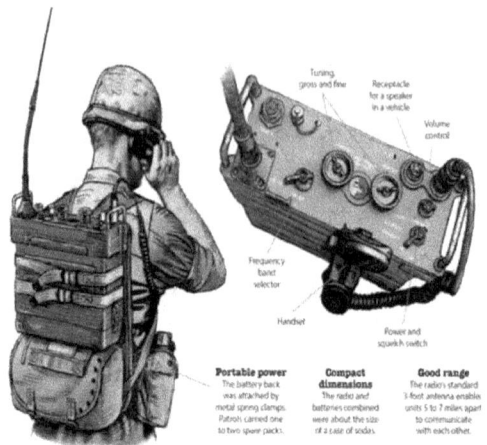

The Most Important Tactical Field Item in the Vietnam War" (www.historynet.com/event/vietnam-war)

Comments from interviewing Frank "Hazel" Farrell: Frank said, "my worst memory as an RTO was when I was providing radio comms for my platoon leadership. Frank conveyed, "I was in the field during a firefight, and out of nowhere, my Communications Chief, SSG Fowler, was hit in the chest with three slugs. There was nothing I could do, as he died even before the medic could arrive."

Vietnam War Casualty Victor Orin Fowler Jr: Staff Sergeant

(From Vietnam War Casualty (honorstates.org)

SSG Victor O. Fowler was an Infantry Communications Chief assigned to the 1st Cavalry Division, 5th Battalion, 7th Cavalry, Headquarters Company. During his service in the Vietnam War, Army Staff Sergeant Fowler experienced a traumatic event that ultimately resulted in the loss of life on October 18, 1966. Incident location: South Vietnam, Quang Tri Province.

SSG Fowler is a Gold Star casualty, and he is honored at the Vietnam Veteran's Memorial in Washington, DC. Name inscribed at VVM Wall, Panel 11e, Line 86.

27 Mar 67

Dear Grandma & Grandpa,

I decided it was about time I drop you a few lines.

Grandma, I didn't mean for you to send me medicine for my sunburn, rashes, and things. The medics have that stuff, but I sure will give yours a try, it's probably better than theirs anyway. I sure do appreciate you going to all that trouble. My lip is better, it's all healed now, but I have to be careful that it doesn't happen again. Seems like when a person gets a sore, it takes twice as long to heal up over here.

I have also received a lot of gum, Kool-Aid, and newspapers. I sure am grateful to you, but you don't have to send them too often, I know it must be costing a lot of money sending them things so often.

You ask what kind of material our roof is made of. Well, everything's wood now, except for the floor, which will be before long. We have a built-in wooden cabinet for the hot plate. All this wood comes from ammo boxes. We tear them down and use the wood out of them. The boards are about 4 feet long.

Sure is hot here, I just sweat sitting around, and don't know how it will be when I start to work.

Well Grandpa, how did you like the way the basketball tournament turned out? Got to admit, Churdan sure must have a good team.

Sorry to hear Daryl has the flu. I sure wish I was there to haul around some manure for him this Spring. Heck, I would even like to slop the hogs. I wonder if he could still use an extra good hand. He's got a lot of help with all those little girls.

Grandpa, I received the picture of the Champion team. Looks like they have plenty of height. If you judge them horse-wise, not bad-looking stock.

Say you mention some coffee, sure, I will pour you a cup, and what about Sparkie? Would he like one of the monkey bananas? He sure brings smoke on dogs, big ones and little ones. We have four dogs that belong to different people around here. Old Joe is always trying to get a free ride on their backs or pulling their tail and

ears. Some guy found Joe in the jungle when he was just a little fella. So he wasn't too hard to tame. Then when he went to the field the guy gave Joe to the Commo section. He doesn't care much for tobacco, but he sure likes beer. He likes bread & eggs the best.

Say Daryl should be getting ready to sell his cattle pretty soon, shouldn't he?

Say, it sounds like you had some excitement when your wild women got away. Must not be too smart if they always get captured. Well, I better close for now.

<u>126 DAYS</u> Leon

5 Apr 67

Dear Grandma & Grandpa,

Well, I reckon it's about time I write you a few lines in response to your most welcome letters and thank you for the comic books, ad gum. Sure do appreciate it.

Well, I was out at LZ Sandra. Got to talk to old Steve V. for a while. His company was resting their a few days. I was just out there for one night to dig in two generators and put in lights for the big wheels. I sure was glad to get out of there, because that place got hit a few days ago. Now I'm back here operating the switchboard again.

Say, I've been using some of that A & D ointment on a rash I got, and it seems to be helping. This sure is an unhealthy place. It seems like I just get one thing cleared up and something else happens.

I got your letter written the 20th of March asking how my home was. Well, the one at LZ Sandra was just a hole in the ground. The one at LZ Pony was a small bunker already built. It was about 8 feet in the ground. When I

went to Sandra, I went by a Sikorsky, that's the big chopper. It flies about 80mph loaded and we were in the air for about 15 minutes. The other time I went, I rode a Huey, and it took about 10 minutes. One thing about being forward, is you get all you can eat, and they usually have plenty of water too.

So, I bet your weather is getting pretty nice back there and the grass should be starting to turn green. It's getting hot here. Yesterday 102 degrees and the day before 100 degrees. The sweat runs 24 hours a day.

Say, Grandma, I sure don't remember ever hoeing for you. You sure must have caught me off guard that day. I sure wouldn't mind hoeing your garden right now.

You mentioned being alone when me and Hazel were out forward at CPAs, there are about 25 guys or more, plus the other units have forward CPs at the same place all the time.

Say, Grandma, sometime when you're sending something, would you throw a few toothpicks in too? I always have something in my teeth and can't ever pick it out. I want to keep them in good shape now that they're all fixed.

Well, better close I guess

<u>118 DAYS</u> *Leon*

Frank Farrell "Hazel," setting up camp at unknown LZ, photo source Frank Farrell

Chapter 12: Steve Streeter and 12th Evac Hospital at Cu Chi

Brother Leon knew Steve Streeter was somewhere in the country and was providing Medic support to the troops based on his Medic training which took place at Ft Sam Houston, Texas, as referenced in Doc Vincent's chapter when they had their car fire during their training.

As alluded to in Leon's letters, he knew Steve Streeter was over in Vietnam somewhere, but he knew he would be ok, as tough as he was. If Leon only knew how Steve's toughness was put to the test on his trip over to Vietnam on the USNS Patrick before he was assigned to the 12th Evacuation Hospital at Cu Chi.

Steve Streeter at Cu Chi, photo source Steve Streeter

A History of the 12th Evac Hospital, Article by Stuart M Poticha, MD, Capt. US Army 1966-1968

The story of my service with the 12th Evacuation Hospital began in 1966, I had completed a five-year residency in General

Surgery at Northwestern University Medical School in Chicago in June 1965, and I was appointed to the surgical faculty and was beginning my surgical practice. One afternoon, as I was finishing rounds, I was paged with a phone call. When I picked up the phone, I heard someone say, "Dr. Poticha, this is Colonel (so and so, I have forgotten or more likely repressed the name). I just wanted to tell you that you are going directly to Vietnam. Don't bring your family, don't bring your car, and don't bring any personal belongings because you are going from basic directly to Vietnam!" "Wait a minute," I said, "You must have the wrong number. I'm not even in the army." "Oh, you haven't received your draft notice yet? Well, that will come tomorrow, but you are going directly to Vietnam. Goodbye. That was my introduction to the United States Army!"

All drafted physicians were sent to Fort Sam Houston in San Antonio for their basic training. So, in February 1966, I arrived at Fort Sam along with several hundred other drafted young docs to learn how to become an Army officer and a battlefield surgeon. Most of the basic training was conducted in lecture halls and was directed at teaching us how to become Army officers. As new draftees, we had to learn the basics, such as which uniform was appropriate at which time, how and where to attach patches, badges, and bars, who and how to salute, and how to march and how to give orders to troops on a march. We even were taught to shoot and had to qualify with a rifle and .45-pistol. The Army realized that we were all physicians who knew how to care for patients, but there were a few specialized medical lectures on the diagnosis and treatment of tropical diseases with strange names such as Dengue Fever, Leptospirosis, Tsutsugamuchi fever, and, of course, malaria.

Civilian surgeons who had trained in large cities were familiar with the management of gunshot wounds, usually from small caliber pistols. Now we were being trained to deal with the high-velocity missiles of war. I remember watching high-powered rifles being shot into blocks of gelatin to show us the widespread damage that this ballistic energy caused to solid tissue.

We were taught the importance of recognizing and excising devitalized tissue in order to prevent infection and a new principle for treating highly contaminated wounds. Instead of closing wounds after they were cleansed, the skin was left open. This allowed the human body's remarkable repair mechanisms to push to the surface any remaining foreign material or dead tissue. After 48 hours, the wounds were again cleansed, and the skin closed.

This technique, called delayed primary closure, markedly reduced the number of infections and saved many lives in Vietnam.

Most importantly, it was in basic training that the 25 or so physicians and surgeons who would form the nucleus of the 12th Evac first came together. Every evening we gathered to tell stories of civilian lives, our training, our families, and, of course, to bitch about the Army. The camaraderie that began at Fort Sam served us well in the coming months in Vietnam. We became a cohesive unit, a dedicated band of docs who could put our egos aside and work together to provide the best possible care for the wounded soldiers we were soon to encounter.

A different story was unfolding for the enlisted men of the 12th. They spent their time inventorying and packing an entire 400-bed hospital with all its equipment supplies and tented housing into an innumerable number of huge steel Conex containers. Finally, after some four months and numerous false alarms, on August 28, 1966, all of the personnel of the 12th Evac in full field uniforms were loaded onto buses and delivered to the Port of Oakland to the rousing music of a naval band as we boarded a ship for our seventeen-day voyage to Vietnam.

The USNS Edwin E. Patrick was a troop transport ship commissioned in January 1945. She was capable of transporting 5,217 troops and all their equipment, but on this voyage, there were only about 2,000 on board. The ship held an extensive medical dispensary that included a fully equipped operating room. Besides the usual shenanigans that took place as we passed the International Date Line and were initiated into King Neptune's Court and the Royal Order of the Golden Dragon, the voyage was memorable for two other events. First, our two-day passage through a Pacific typhoon caused most of us to be so seasick that we weren't even able to move from our bunks, and second, an emergency appendectomy I performed aboard the ship.

Technically the first operation of the 12th Evac's Vietnam history was a simple appendectomy.

The simple appendectomy that Dr. Poticha mentions above is normally a simple procedure, but this emergency appendectomy was anything but simple and was downright scary.

Comments from Interviewing Steve Streeter: Steve said, "I was on my way to Vietnam on the USNS Patrick when I started to have stomach pain, and after a few hours, the pain became so unbearable I decided I better go to the ship infirmary to get something for it. The attending Doc on duty examined me and said I was having an appendicitis attack and I would have to have it removed. He added the ship doesn't have the proper equipment, were not able to do spinal anesthesia, etc., so you will have to wait three days until the ship arrives in Okinawa for the procedure. I was in a lot of pain, so he gave me something for the pain and had two guys help me back to my bunk. As we were going up the stairwell from the infirmary, we ran into Capt. (doctor) Poticha, and he saw how much pain I was in and noted the fact I needed two guys to help me. He said, "Do you mind if I give you another examination? Of course, I said no." He proceeded to examine me and said, "Just as I had feared, your appendix has already burst; if we don't operate now, you could be dead in 24 hours."

Comments from Interviewing Steve Streeter. "Dr. Poticha had me prepped for surgery right away. Since they didn't have the ability to give spinal anesthesia on board, they gave me local anesthesia. They waited about an hour to make sure the local had taken effect and then started cutting on me. The pain was so unbearable I started yelling profanities while raising up on the operating table, breaking both strap restraints they had used to time me down. So, they decided to start giving me additional injections of anesthesia. Not sure how many shots I was given, but it seemed like the procedure took hours to complete, but in reality, it lasted around an hour. After I survived that ordeal, Dr. Poticha and I kind of bonded and became close during my tour at the 12th Evac Hospital."

Although the medical staff had been farmed out to various hospitals across the country, the construction engineers and our enlisted men were busy laying the cement pads and constructing the 54 Quonset-type buildings that formed the hospital. The design of the hospital itself was two parallel rows of buildings separated by about fifty yards of dirt that, in the rainy season, turned into a giant mud pit that could only be crossed by two covered wooden sidewalks. The first row of buildings fronted the helipad and contained emergency pre-op, radiology, two operating room buildings, and three intensive care units. All these Quonset-type buildings were airconditioned.

The OR buildings each contained three small operating rooms separated from each other by curtains. The second row of buildings housed the post-op recovery units and the medical wards.

The doctors and officers were housed in hooches with wooden floors and wooden sides extending upward about 4 ft. Above that were screens, and the whole structure was covered with a canvas tent. Each of the three hooches housed ten cots, five on either side of an aisle that ran down the center of the tent. We partitioned our hooch so that each officer had a tiny private space adjacent to his cot, but others kept the whole space open.

Between each of the hooches, we built our sandbagged rocket and mortar shelters. In late November, all the physicians were recalled to Cu Chi, and the nurses arrived. We received our first casualties on December 4, 1966. The remaining days were a mixture of frantic activity interspersed with long days of boredom. When a helicopter landed, patients were rushed by stretcher to the pre-op hut, where clothes were cut off. As the patients were examined, the severity and location of the wounds were assessed, transfusions and respiratory resuscitation started, and superficial hemorrhage was controlled. Some wounds were horrendous, beyond description. Those patients who were unstable were immediately taken to the ORs. Others were sent to X-ray first.

At times, there were two choppers on the ground unloading patients and several others circling. In mass casualty situations, we might have 50, 60 who knows how many arriving at once. The base itself was frequently attacked by mortar and rocket fire. When that happened, we rushed to the shelters, and as soon as the noise stopped, we ran to pre-op. In mass casualty situations, extra tents were hastily erected around the helipad, and these served as extra ERs and resuscitation centers. Lieutenant Colonel Andy Rusinko, who was Regular Army and the second in command, walked among these wounded men doing triage. Although I was usually operating on patients, on a few occasions, I had to do the triage, and I felt the enormity of that task. Walking down the rows of desperately wounded men, with a glance and cursory exam, deciding who would go to surgery first and who could wait for the next available operating room. It was the hardest job I ever had.

Surgeons worked continuously until all had been cared for, sometimes over 24 straight hours. Patients with massive bleeding from shattered liver or spleens, torn great blood vessels, and even penetrating wounds to the heart were saved. If they got to the hospital alive, our job was to make sure they left alive.

Comments from Interviewing Steve Streeter: Steve said, "I remember one time Dr. Poticha pulled me into one of his delicate surgeries where a soldier had a bullet lodged in his heart. Dr. Poticha conveyed to me later, "Can you believe he's going to be ok even after we had to replace his entire blood volume during the procedure and remove a bullet from his heart." Steve added, "Doc confided in me later that he had saved three additional soldiers who went through basically the same surgery with bullets lodged in their hearts. "Incredible." As I recall later, he said he had received letters from them and their families thanking him for saving their boys." That was a huge morale boost for him to think he was making a difference."

Although huge amounts of blood were needed, unlike in civilian hospitals, there was never a shortage of blood. Some patients had their entire blood volume replaced several times until the hemorrhages could be stopped. Every time a call went out that blood was needed, a long line of volunteers from the 25th Division immediately formed. When the blood reached the operating rooms, it was still warm.

The 12th Evac ended its mission in Vietnam in 1970. During its four years of service, we treated over 37,000 patients. The 12th entered the history books, having treated the most patients with the lowest mortality rate of any hospital in Vietnam.

Comments from Interviewing Steve Streeter. Steve said, "Most of my dental medic time at the 12th Evac was assisting operations for facial, and jaw procedures in the OR, more specifically jaws to include extensive dental restructure. I recall one time we had a young soldier come in with his whole lower jaw shot off, and the doctor spent 18 hours putting his face back together. It was endless; unlike an occasional trauma patient in your civilian emergency room, ours occurred every day, and it really wears on you."

Article featuring Veteran Sarah Blum, a decorated Vietnam Veteran, Author. From The High Ground Newsletter, June 2022, thehighground.us.

Sarah L. Blum, ARNP, is a decorated Nurse Vietnam Veteran, retired nurse psychotherapist, and Author.

Sarah's new book, Warrior Nurse PTSD and Healing, is ready for publication.

The first thing that hit me when I arrived in Vietnam in January 1967 was the incredible heat and smells.

I was one of a couple of hundred nurses arriving at Bien Hoa Air Base searching among the 200 identical olive drab duffle bags for mine as the sweat rolled down my uniform, rolled down my face, and into my eyes. After the ordeal, I was taken on an Army bus with heavy crisscross metal grills over the windows to the 90th replacement battalion. I learned that the window covering was to prevent grenades from coming through. For three days, we learned how to send and receive mail, what Vietnamese money was, and how to get it and get paid. We also learned a bit about the culture and areas where we had hospitals. Finally, we were all assigned to hospitals and sent on our way. I went to the 12th Evacuation hospital at Cu Chi.

The night before I left, I met a drill sergeant from basic training who asked me where I would be sent. When I told him, his face drained of color, and he said, "Get it changed; you don't want to go there. That is the worst place to be; it is where all the fighting is, and it is not safe."

I told him, "I can't change it now because I switched with a young nurse who had the same Military Occupational Specialty (MOS). She was scared and crying because she didn't want to go to Cu Chi. I had been assigned to the 67th Evacuation Hospital at Qui Nhon and offered to switch with her because I wanted to be where the action was. The chief nurse agreed because of the severe emotional distress of the younger nurse. I don't care where I am stationed as long as I can help our soldiers." He was not happy about it at all and told me to keep my head down and stay safe.

My footlocker and duffle bag were taken by a truck, and I was taken by a Huey helicopter to go to the 12th Evacuation Hospital. My first helicopter ride was scary because they did not have doors. I felt very vulnerable sitting in a canvas seat in the wide-open space while flying in a war zone and if you think that was frightening, the landing was worse. When they arrived at the hospital, the helicopter crew would not land the helicopter. They told me I had to jump out onto the helipad. The helicopter is very hard to be heard over the sounds of the rotor blades. I kept pointing down with my arm and finger, "put this thing down," and they kept shaking their heads and said, "jump." They hovered the helicopter about six feet above the helipad but would not land it, and I had to jump. I guess that was my initiation.

Or was? Next, I was saluting our very strict executive officer to find out where to report. He looked starched and professional and did not like my answer to his question, "What is that?" pointing to my ukulele case. I brought a baritone ukulele with me, so I had an instrument to play while there. My answer was a joke to lighten the situation, "It's a machine gun; I thought I might need it over here." That was the wrong thing to say to him, and for the next twenty minutes, he yelled at me for being disrespectful to an officer and finally told me where to report.

Fast forward now to my year there, which included creating a space for me in the hooch, a bed, a closet I made from a large equipment box, and my footlocker and some shelves I made from wood Masonite. I could not stand the smell of the sheets that the Moma San washed, so I took some new green operating room sheets, used them all year, and washed them myself in an extra-large aluminum bowl for washing clothes. Once I completed my personal space, I started working.

We had two Quonset huts for our operating rooms. The main was called Arizona, and in it, we had five different petitioned areas that counted as a room. Each area had an operating room (OR) table, equipment for giving anesthesia, a large stainless-steel table I would use for instruments and sterile supplies for each case, and an over-the-table stand we use during the operation for instruments and supplies like suture materials and extra instruments. We had one shift only, and that was 9 AM until we were done with scheduled cases for the day and then all the cases generated by war. We often worked around the clock, but the average was about 16 hours a day. I was on call for four nights a week.

We had soldiers with wounds all over their bodies or only parts of their bodies. Often, they lost arms, legs, and eyes, or they had shrapnel that tore through major organs in their bodies, which we had to repair. I definitely saw the worst of war and what war does to the land and human beings on it. Yes, we were targets and mortared often. Fortunately, I was never hit, and the worst hit to our hospital occurred the month after I left. After I had been there for about six months, I had a major emotional experience. A young red-headed soldier was hit by American artillery and had the lower half of his body blasted severely. From his hip bones down, he was black, charred, and bleeding. We had four surgeons look at him to decide what they could save and what they could do for him. There were some large skin flaps to cover the remainder of his pelvis. He literally was half a man. I was ok during the surgery because I had learned to be numb to it all, but then on his day three, the day he came into the OR for the closure of his skin flaps, I snapped. He was at one end of the Quonset hut on a stretcher, and I came in from the opposite end. As I walked toward him, I saw the flat sheet covering the stretcher, and half the length of it was flat because there was nothing there. Finally, my eyes saw the bump that was his bandaged hips and then his torso with the sheet, and finally, his face and eyes. My eyes followed all that up to his face, and when

I saw his red hair and blue eyes, something inside me snapped, and I ran out the doors at this end. Some assault helicopters were flying overhead at that moment, and I shouted as loudly as I could through my rage and tears at the choppers, "kill, kill, kill- that is all you know how to do! I hate this war!"

I have no memory of what I did or how long I was going around the hospital yelling at the sky, but I ended up in front of my chief nurse, telling her, "You have to get me out of the OR; I can't take it anymore, put me on the malaria ward or something." She shook her head and said, "I cannot do that; you just need a rest. Take a few days and go down to the beach at Vung Tau and get yourself together."

I drank beer and ate pineapples, had great food, and talked with the Aussies. They were the guys who ran the phone lines in Vietnam, and they were my lifeline. I could talk to them late at night after working 16-18 hours and be able to relax and sleep. In Vung Tau, knowing that I had to go back for more horrors of war, I put a strong wall around my heart to be able to do it. Once back home, in order to heal, I had to take that wall down, and it was not easy.

Chapter 13: Brown Mule 7

A handwritten letter by Leon Toyne, "Brown Mule 7."

16 Apr 67

Dear Grandma & Grandpa,

I received your two more comic books and a funny paper yesterday, so thought I would write you a few lines, and tell you I sure do appreciate it. I kind of get a kick out of reading those comic books and always enjoy the funny papers.

Say, I'm sending a special picture of me building a bunker. This is taken from a Polaroid camera Nick has. If you would like some more pictures, I would have to send for some more film for it. They don't sell that kind of film it uses out here. Nick's mother sends it to him.

Everybody has moved out, but about 45 of us are left back to man the bunkers. Me and old Swamp Rat, run this switchboard 24 hours a day now, so we don't get a lot of sleep. I can't sleep in the daytime, so I am running pretty low on sleep. The battalion went back to An Khe for a 10-day rest. We have such a good position dug in here, so they hated to leave and let somebody move in, so we are just kind of watching over the equipment and bunkers.

I was sure glad to hear Dad went into the hog business, that gives the Men something to do.

Grandpa, you ask about Old Nitro. They got him out forward operating the generators for power to run the

radios. Never see him much. Nick is the kid that's been with me ever since I've been in the Army. He and Hazel both are from Wisconsin.

I got lots of time to write but never can think of anything to say. The switchboard isn't very busy since about everybody's gone.

Guess I will have to close for now.

<u>*106 DAYS*</u> *Leon*

Brown Mule 7 building a bunker with sandbags At LZ Pony, photo source Leon Toyne family

18 Apr 67

Dear Grandma & Grandpa,

This is "Brown Mule 7" opening up the net for traffic for your station at this time. This is Bird Dog 8.

So, pull up a chair, and have a shot of my old rusty coffee and we will send a little traffic over our nets. By the way, I get so If I drink enough of the old rusty coffee, I can stay awake better.

I hope you don't have anything important right now to do because I got 5 hours of nothing to do but send a little traffic over your network.

My working hours kind of changed now. I work from 1:00 in the morning to 7:00 in the morning. Then I get 6 hours off and then go on another 6 hours. Most of the time I read books, play cards, and curse the Army.

Joe isn't around here now. So, it's pretty dull. Harry is back from RR, so he takes care of Ole Joe. Happy is here, though he's little company. Anyway, he visits long enough to eat. I think he kind of misses Old Joe pulling his ears and riding his back. I'm afraid Ole Joe would be a hard pull for Sparkie because Joe can whip about any dog around here.

Sounds like Daryl must be pretty busy. Sounds like by the way he's been tearing out fences, and plowing. He isn't going to save any work at all

for me to help with. Maybe he will run into Bruce's fence again and I could put a post in or something.

Say, Grandpa, these new iron horses never will replace the old team, will they? You never hear of a horse blowing a head gasket.

Say, not to change the subject or anything, but you're going to have to invite me up for dinner sometime. I get tired of this SOS they pass out here. That means the same old slop.

Well, due to a pour transmission and a lot of static, I'm afraid I will have to close this net for tonight. This is "Brown Mule 7" going off the frequency.

104 DAYS Leon

22 Apr 67

Dear Grandma & Grandpa,

I have received two packages in two days, so decided I better get in gear, and tell you how much I really appreciate it. Those toothpicks sure do help to pick my teeth. My old scrub brush wasn't wearing out yet, but it's good to have a spare. I'll have to try that new kind of toothpaste, and see how it does. We get Crest & Colgate here, and this other might be better.

Never mind about that film I mentioned. I found a place that sells that type of film.

Well, let's see, I'm still operating this Damm switchboard 12 hours a day. Don't have time for much of anything else, besides a little sleep now and then.

Say, I got a good picture of me, and ole Swamp. He's from New York, He's just a pretty good old buddy. There's just me and ole Swamp operating this switchboard. One thing with just a few of us out here, they don't bother us much. I got a call from old Billy T. early this morning. Say old Hazel's on KP, she sure hates that, glad I stayed out here. They're supposed to be coming back out here from An Khe Sunday, so our freedom is about over.

Well, can't seem to think of any more traffic to send you at this time, so will close for now.

100 DAYS Leon

Chapter 14: Guarding the Dump

27 Apr 67

Dear Grandma & Grandpa,

Well, I'll try and take a little time to answer your two most welcome letters, which I received a few days ago.

Grandpa was glad to hear you got the tobacco. I hope they didn't charge you any tax on it. We get that tobacco in our 101 rations, and hardly anyone smokes a pipe over here, so there's a lot of it thrown away. It might not be the freshest, but I thought you might get some good out of it.

I got a job guarding a road that leads to the trash dump, and it sure isn't a boring job. Yesterday an ARVN troop, that's a Vietnamese soldier, shot a little girl in the shoulder, just to show off, I guess. Then, the day before, they shot a water can off a mule. The day after that, they threw gas on some kids and made the kids pretty sick. I had to call civil affairs, but they never seem to catch them at it or do anything to prevent it. I have a gate on the road that I control, for keeping the kids from coming through. So far 14 days and my job aren't boring at all, because there is always something happening every day.

A company sends guards down to me at night to pull guard, but I have to be here by myself all day long. Right across the fence from me is this old Papa San, he's got the old cows plowing up this ground. He's got old Moma San leading them for him, quite a site to see.

Grandma, I like them funny books, and they sure do get used. About a dozen different people read them when I'm done. Even my old Platoon Sergeant asks me if my Grandma sent any new comic books.

You mention the water. It doesn't taste too bad if it doesn't set in those rubber bladders too long. I usually fill two to three 5-gallon cans before they set in the sun too long. You mentioned Steve V. I haven't seen him since I was out an LZ Sandra, that's been about a month ago. We got two new replacements in our wire section now, so we got more help so I don't have to work so hard. That other bunker we built was for the extra wireman. Those that are here now that weren't before.

I don't see where I can get out of here before August. I'd be darn lucky to get out then probably. Well, due to TT traffic at this time, I will be forced to close the net.

94 DAYS Leon

Comments from interviewing Frank "Hazel" Farrell: Frank said, "It was difficult guarding the dump against all the Vietnamese children. They were always begging for food because they were so hungry.

Occasionally, we would give them leftover C-Rations, but that increased the problem because they would tell more kids, and then you'd be overrun by them. If you left your post or bunker unattended, they'd take your stuff."

29 Apr 67

Dear Grandma & Grandpa,

I received your most welcome package yesterday. That is the right film. However, I only got two pictures out of it. The camera wasn't set right, I didn't know until four of them got ruined. I got two here, and one isn't too

clear. The kid taking it didn't know how to set the camera. You can also see they got some dirt on them before they dried. That chopper on the picture just took off and blew dirt on them, Say, I kind of like those little cigars. I sure want to thank you for them and the film. You don't have to send any more film, since they sell it at the PX and it's cheaper here.

When the battalion came back from ten days of rest, they left Little Joe the monkey back at An Khe in the motor pool, so I don't have much company now at the guard bunker. The little dog we had got gassed, so we had to put him to sleep.

Right now, there are a half dozen kids by the gate yacking like a bunch of magpies. I just bought a coke from one of them, and the rest are all mad because I never bought their coke. My bunker is only about 25 yards from old Papa San's house. He's got 12 kids so you can imagine how it is around there, never a dull moment. Only three of his kids are boys, the rest are girls.

Well, here it is another day, so will try to get this letter finished today.

Steve V. came in from the field yesterday. He came down to visit for a couple of hours and to put in for another R&R. He seems to be doing fine. They aren't doing a lot of humping like before. Sweeping a few villages during the daytime, but holding up mostly at night.

I sure am having a hard time finishing this letter. I sit on top of the roof of my bunker so I can watch the road better. The chopper pad is right behind my bunker, and every time a chopper takes off, I have to get off my roof so he won't blow me away.

Well, I guess I will bring this to a close, due to no further traffic for you, closing the net for now.

<u>93 DAYS</u>   Leon

4 May 67

Dear Grandma & Grandpa,

I received the newspapers and gum a few days ago. Don't feel that the papers aren't worth sending, because anything that's happening back in the states is interesting news to me. I hope you don't mind dirty paper and envelopes. These choppers blow dirt all over everything every time they land here at the pad.

Now let's get back to the little chat, and a cup of this rotgut coffee. I call it coal oil, that's what it tastes like and I've never tasted coal oil either. I think this stuff would burn like coal oil.

Well, here I am again, the sweat started to run so I had to quit. Right now, it's just turning daylight, so will try to get off a few lines before it gets too hot.

You know the rooster's crow here, just like they do back in the states when it's getting daylight, but the feeling is still different.

Well, last night I went back to the switchboard bunker, played cards, and ate popcorn for a couple of hours. On this sleeping business. If I get 6 hours, I can go the next night without hardly any sleep. Six hours is the most I get at any one time. I'm getting pretty well used to it, but if I get the chance, I sure could sleep all night with no trouble at all.

These pictures you mentioned seeing at LZ English. Well, that's about ½ mile from where I'm probably. You also asked about "Brown Mule 7", well that's my little joke. Each net on the radio has its own call sign, so I made up one for my own. When you are calling some other net, you say "Warpoint 4" this is "Bold Eagle", over. Then he comes back and says this is "Bold Eagle", then "Warpoint 4" sends his message.

Sounds like $50.00 an acre is a lot of money for corn, but maybe not, don't know that much about it.

Sure sounds like Dad is really fixing things up. I hope that the hog project pays off. Grandma, so your wild women pulled a railroad job. A pretty smart way to make a getaway.

Well, they have started to transfer us to different outfits. Hazel is supposed to leave in a few days. They will be taking one at a time until our rotation date. So, I guess after all this time we can't be together.

That bunker you ask about had a tent inside it, and those sandbags were just the walls. The tent has been taken down now, and a big bunker is built. I don't use an alarm clock, because I sleep so light. I don't need one. I don't think Joe will grow anymore. He's still in An Khe. Joe really drinks, he is a real old boozer.

That planter Daryl bought must be a good one. I'll have to have a few words with old Unk, he didn't even consult me before he got it. That kind of money sure would buy some good-blooded horses.

I'm almost 20 yards from the village and all kinds of good-looking girls. I've been proposed to so many times already. A total of 449 GIs married Vietnamese girls and took them back to the states.

Well, Grandpa, I think the press is pretty used up, so will close for now.

<u>87 DAYS</u>   Leon

Chapter 15: Transferring from 5th Bn/7th Cav - Building Barracks

14 May 67

Dear Grandma & Grandpa,

I guess I better write you and tell you my address has changed. I no-longer belong to 5/7. I was transferred out of there two days ago. I sure did hate to leave but knew it would happen, but I didn't think so soon. Before August, everybody but a few of the old guys will be transferred to other units. Steve V. was transferred the same day I was. He went to the 87th Engineers.

You mentioned Swamp Rat, he's from New York, Nick's from Wisconsin and he's about 6ft 1in, so there's a little difference between him and Swamp Rat. Hazel isn't a girl, we just call him Hazel because he worries about everybody, but himself, his real name is Frank Farrell. **(Frank's RTO call sign was Hazel).**

That picture of me and Mike, we were holding M-16s. Now in this new unit, they gave me an M-79 grenade launcher. I don't even think I can fire it. Wish I had an M-16 again.

So, Daryl is going into the horse business. Sounds like a really pretty stallion he bought.

They're sending me out to LZ Dog, that's right near LZ English. I sure will be glad to get out in the field again. They're having an inspection tomorrow, and I sure hate them. I should stay out there till I rotate; I hope.

I sure do look forward to your letters, because it sure is lonesome here when you don't know anybody. So, at night I sit up and read my letters over several times. I sure want to thank you for the cigars. I tried to send some more tobacco, but they won't let me do it anymore. Some kind of law that I can't send it to the States.

Well, can't seem to think of much more to say. Maybe I will have something to say that's interesting in my next letter. I should know more about this place by then.

<u>78 DAYS</u>   Leon

21 May 67

Dear Grandma & Grandpa,

I've received two welcome letters from you since I've written, so thought it was time I drop you a few lines. I also got the funny paper and comic book. I want to thank you a million for them.

Well, I have a permanent job now. I'm a carpenter. I work with a crew that goes around building barracks. We work 6 ½ days a week, and we get Sunday morning off. We work from 7:30 in the morning until 6:30 in the evening, with an hour off for dinner. So, you can see, we get in some pretty good hours. One of the things that made me take this job is they started to put me on KP, right then I asked for this job because you don't pull any other duty. Besides, it will help me get in shape when I finally do get ready to work when I get out of here. I'll be doing this until I rotate. They don't have a place for me in the field, and I don't have a long time left. I won't have to worry about helicopters blowing my papers off now, because I live in a barracks.

No need to send any film for a swing camera, because no one here has one. The guy in the picture with me is Mike M., Nick is about 6ft 2in. Mike is a wireman.

I sure would like to get out early, but by the time everything was fixed, it would probably be time for me to get out anyway. The R&R doesn't make any difference in getting out. It's just rest from duty that doesn't count as leave time. If there was a chance of getting out next month, I sure would give it a try.

Grandma, you better take care of those bad headaches, I hope you will feel better soon.

Sure glad that Dad is having good luck with the pig project. Grandma, my mouth sure watered when you went down to the folks and had cake and ice cream.

You ask about the Vietnamese. Their skin is the color of an Indian. I think the hot summer has a lot to do with the tanning brown because the really small kids are pretty light-colored. They are really small people. A boy here at the age of 18 looks the size of age eleven in the States. I really don't see how they work it if somebody marries one of the women. I think everything is free as long as you're in the service. They are getting to the place where they can speak our language a little, and it's easier for us to get across what we want. I can hardly wait to get a look at the stallion Daryl bought. I know what he means, shipping fever. Once I bought a horse and it gave distemper to all the rest.

Well, no more hot plates or rusty coffee. They do have a coffee break around here at 9:00 in the morning, and at 2:00 in the afternoon, but usually we don't stop working.

You ask about roosters. They look like bunnies and are all colors. They have a lot of hens and the villagers raise them to eat and sell at markets in the towns.

Well, maybe I should bring this to a halt, until next time.

<u>71 DAYS</u>   Leon

24 May 67

Dear Grandma & Grandpa,

Wow! I sure have been receiving a lot of mail from you, and it makes me feel right down good. I got the box of candy which I'm still enjoying. Two packages of comic books, and newspapers. You don't have to send me so much, because I know this is costing you money, and money is hard to come by nowadays. I'm right near the PX, so I can get a lot of reading material, but I still like the funny papers and things, and I sure do thank you.

If you can't read this too well, it's because my finger hurts. I hit it with a hammer this morning while putting siding on a building. It's turning a little black now.

Say you got anything cold to drink? I don't want any more rusty coffee. How about some cold H2O? Grandpa, when does Lake City school get out? Your track season should be over pretty soon, shouldn't it? How did Lake City's track team do this season?

It's now 1400 hours, so will sign off for now and take this up again at 2100 hours if possible.

Well, here I am back again, and I haven't done much exciting to talk about. Just work on building a barracks. We are getting ready to put the tin on the roof next. These buildings are only supposed to last 5 years, then they will tear them down if they haven't fallen down, then build another. The cement over in this climate doesn't last 5 years, and the same way with the lumber. It's pretty poor-grade lumber too.

I sure hope they leave me on this job and we don't run out of work in the next two months. I guess tomorrow I heard they will be pulling us from this detail to go on an LRP for a day, which I sure don't care for.

Well, my time sure is getting short, but it seems like now the times going really slow. I guess because I hear where all this harassment is. Well, till we exchange traffic again, so long for now.

<u>69 DAYS</u>   Leon

29 May 67

Dear Grandma & Grandpa,

I've received three letters from you and I've decided I better write, or you might think I was ailing. Sure nice to get mail again, for about four days I didn't get any.

I get to sleep all night without getting up, and it sure feels good not to have to get up in the middle of the night. We get up at about 5:30 every morning and I'm always awake before then. An alarm clock would be just a waste of money for me. I have my own built-in.

They do have horses over here and they are pretty poor lookers. Mostly all Shetlands pulling two-wheeled carts. In the village of An Khe, they use a pony and a cart for taxis.

Grandma, if your press isn't working too good, give it a shot of oil. Ha!

Grandpa, how many acres of corn did Daryl plant this year? I got to get busy and drop him a few lines. Sounds like Daryl will be busy for a while, as he starts farrowing 40 sows.

Sounds like your weather is getting real nice out your way. Wasn't too bad here yesterday, as it was 97 degrees. We don't have any apple trees, but got plenty of bananas.

So, the old prison is a little on the dull side here lately? What do they have, their own ball games among themselves?

Sounds like Dad could handle many more pigs if he has to use oats bins.

Well, I'm starting to get to know guys around here now. There are only around 25 in this company here now.

The rest are at LZ Dog, so I don't know how many there are for sure. The company has 14 gunships now. I guess I told you I'm at Camp Radcliff, An Khe. I'm done in the field. I'm just waiting my turn to go. I'm inside the perimeter, so don't have to worry about getting shot at here. I sleep inside a barracks in a bed too.

I know how to shoot that M-79 now. It looks like a sawed-off shotgun. It's a lot more deadly than an M-16. It shoots a round about 3 inches long and about 1 ½ inches wide.

I haven't heard from Nick or the other guys. I'm getting to know a lot of guys now, so it isn't so bad. With this new job, I still don't pull any KP, and of course, I sure will do anything possible not to pull it.

So, you need some rain. Well, it's dry here too, as it doesn't rain anymore until August or later.

AVN means aviation organization in a flying unit. Our company has 14 gunships, that's helicopters, that don't carry troops, just equipped with weapons.

Steve V.'s company is just a little way down the road from me, but I haven't seen him since I got into this company. Well, I hope you get some rain soon. Guess I better bring this to a close

<u>64 DAYS</u>   Leon

31 May 67

Dear Mom, Dad & All,

Mom, I received your welcome letter a couple of days ago, so will try and drop you a few lines before I go to work this morning.

I sure do like my job. I only hope I can keep it till I rotate. I'm supposed to, but in the Army that doesn't mean a thing. We are getting ready to start another building. We built forms and rafters yesterday and the day before.

I sure am glad to hear your pig project is coming along real good, Dad. I heard you had so many you had to put them in the oats bin. I sure would like to see the place, can hardly wait, but one of these days real soon I should be around that way. You should have plenty of help now with the Men out of school. It makes me a little more homesick, being in this unit and not knowing guys too good. I met a guy from Newton, Iowa. There's one from Colorado. The rest are New York, California, and big places like that.

Say before I forget, don't send that baking soda if you haven't yet. Since I've been inside the camp, I can take a shower every night. I have finally got rid of my rash. Never mind, I just received another letter from you today. Sorry, you already sent the baking powder, but I'll find some use for it.

I sure am tired tonight. We had action out on the Green-Line last night. So today, we had to go out and make a sweep of the area, we didn't find anything so I'll be back to my carpenter work in the morning.

You ask how far I am from An Khe. Well, I guess Camp Radcliff is about 2 miles from An Khe. I'm about a mile from my old Camp Radcliff unit. All the guys in this unit are trained to fly helicopters, mostly.

Sounds like you men are real athletes. Did you win the race?

I haven't heard anything or seen Steve V. He could be back in the field.

Glad to hear Bruce likes the pickup, maybe I can sell him another one someday. Sure hope your poor old farmers get some rain for your crops. I hear it got clear up to 97 degrees there a few days ago. Takes a lot of water for stock when it's that hot. Well, guess I better sign off and get this letter sent.

<u>61 DAYS</u>   Leon

2 Jun 67

Dear Grandma & Grandpa,

How is everything in the world? I hope you have some rain by now, or the crops will be getting pretty thirsty.

I received your package of cigars a couple of days ago, so really been making a lot of smoke here lately. Also got the funny papers and comic book. I sure enjoy them. I don't know how I'll ever repay you for all these nice things you have sent me.

Yesterday, I ran into old Swamp Rat when I was working, he's the short guy in the picture, and his real name is Mike. He told me Hazel, Gill, Doug, and a couple of others have been transferred. The old HHQ company mail clerk is in A company of this battalion. I ran into him yesterday too. I guess the way Mike talked, Nick might stay in the old unit. It sure was good to see Mike, he's in the 207th.

They do have bunkers beside the barracks when there is a mortar attack.

You asked about Steve V. I still haven't seen him. He might be around here, or maybe in the field, but I don't think they would have sent him to the field. His battalion is about a ½ mile from mine.

Sounds like you really got some warm weather the other day. I bet the livestock around the country took a lot of water that day.

Sounds like the student must be pretty rough on equipment to tear up that big of a bill. Well, got started in June now, so times moving along, but still seems slow.

I guess I'll have to bring this to a close and go drive some nails.

<u>59 DAYS</u>   Leon

8 Jun 67

Dear Grandma & Grandpa,

I received a letter from you today, and all kinds of good things all week long, so decided I better write you a letter and let you know I really appreciate it.

Say, I bought myself one of those Swinger cameras the other day. Now I'm waiting for the PX to get some film, and I'll send you a picture or two.

I guess I better tell you what LRP means. It is Long Range Patrol. That means going out in the jungle and making sweeps for VC, and traps. The sweep is over now. We only went 9000 meters. We were back by supper time. The jungle sure was thick and hot.

Hey, my thumbnail turned a little black, but it doesn't hurt anymore.

It's been raining a little every day, so it isn't too hot. They have a big refrigerator in the NCO barracks, so we get cold sodas once in a while.

When does your first baseball game start? I suppose it's already started by this time.

Well, today I'm nailing siding on a building. It looks like we got a lot of barracks to put up yet.

I still haven't heard or seen anything of Steve V. I doubt if I ever do with the kind of job I got. It keeps me busy and I don't have time to go very far. Once and a while I do slip away and see a movie in the evening.

Well, let's see if I can think of more traffic for you. My press is in good shape and I just need something to run through it.

Here it is evening, and I'm still working on this letter that I started this morning. So here I am, just fired up one of those King Edwards cigars you sent me. Can't think of anything to say, because I do the same thing every day now.

How's old Sparkie doing? We have a dog here we call Tony. He's kind of a brown spotted color and hangs around the supply room most of the time, but he never misses a formation. There are other dogs, but Tony belongs to D Company.

Everybody has a nickname. In my old outfit, they call me the "Prairie Dog Kid". One kid in here they call Toad because he looks and moves like one.

These past four or five days the weather hasn't been hot at all, because it's rained a little every day. I'm sure glad I'll be out of here before the monsoon season starts.

Well just cannot think of anything worth saying, so will close for now.

<u>52 DAYS</u>   Leon

12 Jun 67

Dear Mike,

I got your welcome letter a few days ago. So decided I better drop your old bacon a few lines.

Glad to hear your old pig is growing a little. Better feed him extra good, because the more he weighs, the more money you will get when you sell him.

Glad to hear you won a few ribbons. Must have some good running blood in your old veins.

I got a friend and his name is Toad, he works on the construction job with me, and he's real funny. You would sure get a kick out of him. He's short, and he looks a little like a toad.

I hear you and everybody sure been fixing up the place. I hear Daryl gave you and Steve a pony to ride. How do you like him or her? Do you ride much?

I'm still pounding nails, so I don't have anything very interesting to write about.

Well old Innertube, I cannot think of a thing to say to your old bacon. So will have to shut this letter off, due to no traffic to transmit to your station at this time.

<u>*49 DAYS*</u> *Leon*

12 Jun 67

Dear Steve,

I received two welcome letters from you, so I thought I better get busy and answer them. Sounds like you and Mike did all right winning ribbons. Must be just pretty fast runners.

That whiteboard fence sounds real fancy. Sounds like you and Mike are going to have plenty to keep you busy this summer. Too bad I'm not there to help you. I'm getting pretty good at building things now. Steve, you're getting to be a pretty well-experienced hand. Shouldn't be hard for you to get a job.

I suppose you are glad school is out, now you should have a lot of time to improve the old homestead. Sure am looking forward to seeing it. I will probably have to go to Lander first and take care of my business. Then I should be able to spend a little time with your old bacon

How is that little old pony you got to ride? Is he lazy or pretty active?

Well, old Steve I cannot just think of a darn thing to say. I don't do anything interesting now that I'm back in the rear area. So will close for now, and try to do better next time.

<u>*49 DAYS*</u> *Leon*

Chapter 16: Injured – A Long Road to Recovery

17 Jun 67

The American Red Cross Letter (dictated by Leon)

Dear Mom, Dad & All,

Well, I had a little accident. Got hit on the head. I got a minor skull fracture. Right now, I'm in a hospital in the Philippines. They flew me in this afternoon from Piu Nhon. That's a little South of An Khe. They didn't mess around, as soon as I got hurt, they flew me to Quan Huong, special doctors there. The next day they flew me here. Now they will either send me to Japan or home, but don't get your hopes up about the home part. I have never seen the Army do anything in my favor yet. I know in the morning; I'm leaving for somewhere. You better spread the word because this is the only envelope I got.

Now, I just got another shot, and my old butt is full of holes, till it's just like a pin cushion. Another thing, I would beat this letter home probably. I'll let you know more later.

Leon

Leon Toyne injured in combat action

Mr and Mrs Merritt Toyne of Churdan received word that their son, SP/4 Leon Toyne, was injured near An Khe in Vietnam on June 16. During his treatment, Toyne was hospitalized in Qhe Khnon and the Philippines. He is now in Okinawa where he will undergo brain surgery. He has been in Vietnam since August 1966, serving with the 7th Cavalry as a wireman.

His address is SP/4 Leon E. Toyne, US55808833, U. S. Army Hospital, Ryukya Island, APO 96331, San Francisco, Calif.

Jefferson Herald, June 28, 1967, Pg 1, Jefferson Iowa

22 Jun 67

The American Red Cross Letter (dictated by Leon)

Dear Mom, Dad & All,

Well, they sent me to Okinawa, so it might be a while before I get home.

I just got checked over by the doctor a little while ago. I guess that little jolt was worse than I thought. The doctor said I might have to have another operation, and have a plate put in my head, if either they had to cut much more bone, or too much dirt got into the brain.

I got some more news that hurts me a little. I won't be getting out in August now. Just when this happened, I got my orders that said I would be discharged no later than 4 August. Now that I'm here those orders don't mean a thing. The only way that would work is if I got back to Vietnam, and they already said I won't be going back, so now I'll be sent back to the states and re-stationed until I get out in October.

I guess bad luck just follows me around.

Well, there really isn't much more that I can tell you. I'll probably be re-assigned in the states in a couple of weeks. Don't worry about me, I'm in safe hands.

Sure is a lousy way to celebrate a birthday in the hospital, but I guess I will.

Have you received any word that I have left Vietnam outside of me telling you? Here's my current address.

Leon

SP/4 Leon E. Toyne, U.S. 55808833

U.S. Army Hospital Ryukyu Islands

APO 96331 San Francisco, CA

28 Jun 67

Dear Grandma & Grandpa,

I finally got my mail. I was really glad to get your most welcome letters and birthday card. I haven't received the package yet, but it will probably show up before long. Looks like I'll have plenty of time to write now.

I had a little talk with the doctor this morning. Looks like I'll be in this hospital for a long time. He is encouraging me to get this plate put in my head. I don't have to, but he said I should for safety. It cannot be done for about two months when it heals up. So, if I get it, it's done in the states. I am starting to feel really good now. They really feed me well here, just like a café. You order whatever you want. I've gained a little weight back.

I'm up to 160 lbs again. All I do is, eat, sleep, and read books.

You mentioned you hoped I'd spend my birthday in a safe place, well I guess this hospital is about the safest place there is.

This guy that told you AVN means Advise Vietnamese is crazy. It means Aviation, that's Aircraft, and Air Mobility Unit. You travel by air only.

Glad to hear the farmers finally got their rain. Sounds like they are getting plenty of it now.

You ask about the size of the buildings I was building. They are 20 ft wide and 100 ft long. I worked with a crew of six, but I won't have to go back there again.

About LZ English, I was sure glad I left there too. The ammo pit blew up. I was in the hospital with some guys that got hurt from it. It sure did tear up a lot of GIs.

You ask what old Swamp Rat is doing, well he's building barracks like I was.

I heard Steve S. might be getting out soon. I didn't know he was due to get out yet. Wish I could find a way to get out of here.

I cannot think of any more to say, so I better close. Thank you for the birthday card.

? DAYS

Leon

28 Jun 67

Dear Mom, Dad & All,

They finally got my mail transferred here to the hospital. Sure was a welcome sight.

Well, I talked to the doctor this morning. He said I should have a plate put in my head for safety, but I don't have to if I don't want it. If I do get his plate put in my head. I'll have to wait about two months before I can put it in my head because my head has to heal up first. It would be done in the states, so looks like I might stay here until the 1st of August. Then be sent back to the states for the operation.

I lost a little weight, but I'm gaining it back now. They feed me really well here. It's just like a café, and you order what you want.

I'm sleeping in bed with a mattress, wow, what a change, sure feels good.

I have a buddy from Denver, Colorado. We talk about the good country a lot. He wants me to come to see him when I get out.

Dad, I hope you feel better from the flu. So, you sold the pigs. Do you think you got a good price for them? $15 sounds kind of low, but I don't know much about the pig market. That should give you boys rest with just a few pigs to take care of.

Say you boys got a bridle for that pony. You should just make you one from a workhorse bridle or something till I get the one I got.

If you boys shoot that 22 rife, you better be careful you don't have an accident. Glad to hear old Tudy is a good sow dog. She must be a better dog than I thought.

On second thought, maybe you better go ahead and buy a bridle, I don't have any idea when I'll be home.

I tell you one thing if I had it to do all over again. I would join the Air Force because the Army leaves too many scars on a person.

Well, guess I'll close for now Leon

1 Jul 67

Dear Grandma & Grandpa,

I received your most welcome packages of candy, newspapers, and cards. I sure do thank you for the mail and candy.

Well, I guess I better tell you how the little accident happened. The Company Commander picked a place for his quarters to live where there was a lot of brush and rocks, so we had to clear the area before we could put a building there. We set a bunch of charges to clear the place. When the charges went off, I got hit by a rock or something from the blast.

I feel all right now. I have to be operated on again and a plate put in my head, so I won't have a hole in it. A special brain surgeon has to do this, so I'll be flown to the States for the operation. I will probably be in this hospital until the 1st of August and then fly back for the operation then.

I guess I'm lucky I'm still here to talk about it, but it still makes me mad. I'm sure I won't be paying for this operation because it costs about $9000 on the outside. Really wouldn't need the second operation, but the doctors said it would be safer to have it in case I ever get hit there again. He said he will graft skin on my head so there won't be a scar there and a hole. I will be just as good as I was before when it's over. I got a pretty tough head, I guess.

Thank you for all the things you sent. I don't need anything, I guess. This hospital has all kinds of things in it. PX, library, movies, but it's still boring here.

Leon

5 Jul 67

Dear Grandma & Grandpa,

I received your wonderful packages and birthday cards yesterday. I sure do thank you for them real good cookies and cigars, but I can't smoke them. Somebody else might like them, so they won't be wasted.

I don't see how I'll ever get a pension, because I was on a detail at the time, but I will be on the lookout for one.

Don't send me any more mail here, because I'm being sent to the states next week or sooner. An Air Evac is leaving Saturday and I might be on that.

Well, I can't think of any more to write. Tell everybody not to send any more mail, because I won't be here. I'll write my new address later.

Leon

P.S. Thank everyone for the nice cards and things for me. I got 14 letters yesterday too.

13 Jul 67

Dear Grandma & Grandpa,

I've been receiving your wonderful letters, and newspapers every day now, and sure does brighten my day.

They let me run around the hospital. I play ping pong, and cards, and read books. We have the TV too, but it doesn't come on until the afternoon. I try to keep myself occupied, but it's sure hard, day after day.

The doctor tells me every day I'm going home soon, but he's told me that for the past two weeks.

Right after I got hurt, I slept for three days. It sure did feel good to sleep in a real bed. Now I'm getting a little tired of this soft life.

That picture you mention in the paper is probably a picture of this hospital.

Iowa sure must have lousy weather, first, you dry up, and then swim in the water, and now you get hailed on. Best to move to the good country.

Well, I better close, have nothing to say, that's worth saying, Leon

18 Jul 67

Dear Grandma & Grandpa,

I'm still here. I will be here until the 25th of July. That's what the Doc said, and he already sent my papers down for processing, so I guess this is affirmative.

They shipped my baggage to me, and I lost about $100 worth of equipment on the deal, but I guess I was lucky to get any of it. I did get my camera, radio, and banking papers so were glad about that.

How is everybody getting along in the flat country? I'm getting along as well as can be expected in this place. A lot of people sure did send me cards. Some of them I didn't even know. The first mail I got here, there were over 20 letters, sure nice people.

How is the prison? Are the wild women pretty wild, or have you got them tamed down this summer?

So, you say old Sparkie doesn't feel too hot? Sorry to hear that, maybe you should give him a pep pill. That's what they do to the dogs in Vietnam when they get tired.

Here it is morning, and I still haven't finished this letter. Shouldn't be too boring today, I have to go to the dentist, and get some work done on my teeth. So, you know I must feel pretty good.

Will close for now.

Leon

29 Jul 67

Dear Grandma & Grandpa,

I'm sorry I didn't call you, but I don't have a penny, let alone a dime. When I called Dad that was a free call that the Red Cross made for me.

I'm here in this hospital in Denver now. Fitzsimons, they call it. They are running a bunch of tests on me now.

The doctor looked at me and said he wanted to wait a year before he operated because he's afraid of

inflammation if he operates now. So, I'm afraid they are going to re-station me, even with only 90 days left until my ETS in October. The dirty bastards.

No use for you and the folks to come here, because I'll probably only be here a week at the most.

Leon

8 Sep 67

Dear Grandma & Grandpa,

I decided it was time I drop you a few lines, and thank you for the card.

It didn't take long for them to find me a job. They have me doing janitor work.

I see the VA man today. It's all set up for my operation in the Des Moines hospital, and they will send my medical record there. I can't have the operation before 8 July. That's how long you have to wait for plastic surgery for it to do a good job after the wound was made.

Now I might get out before October. They have been doing paperwork on me, but I haven't got my hopes up, because I've had so many disappointments.

They moved me out of the main hospital building to building 509 now.

I also got your letter with $5.00 in it. I'll pay you back when I can, but it may be a while.

Leon

Leon Toyne had a long recovery. He was admitted to Fitzsimons Army Hospital on 22 June 1967 and released on 15 September 1967. Throughout his recovery process, he had extensive medical treatment, which required a total of eight operations. The operations included sensitive brain surgery to remove dirt.

Approximately one year after the injury, in July 1968, he had his final operation to put a plate in his head to cover the large hole in his skull.

Chapter 17: The Non-Welcome Home – The Enemy Within

What my brother Leon endured in Vietnam and how he was able to survive was attributed to his positive attitude and mental and physical toughness. The Vietnam experience was very traumatic. I remember as a kid when he came home, he was a different person. He didn't want to talk about the Vietnam experience, and he buried it in his memory for years, which is why we didn't discover his Vietnam letters until 52 years later after he passed away at 73.

Like many combat veterans, Leon exhibited Post Traumatic Stress Disorder (PTSD) symptoms. I'm sure multiple operations which included brain surgery from his Vietnam injury, contributed to the difficult adjustment and PTSD symptoms, but for the most part, he was able to live a normal life due to his wonderful wife Amie, to whom he was married for 48 years. She provided the love, understanding, and support he needed to effectively manage his PTSD. They raised three great kids on a cattle ranch in Wyoming through determination, hard work, and faith.

The majority of the individuals that went to Vietnam were non-volunteer draftees into the Army from the ages of 18-21. They honorably served and were dedicated to doing the best job they could. When they returned from Vietnam, they became our forgotten heroes. They didn't receive a welcome home parade or any congratulatory recognition like other war veterans from WWI, WWII, The Korean War, Iraq, and Afghanistan; even though they did everything Uncle Sam had asked of them. It was just the opposite. They were not recognized and were treated horribly, even spat on and called names when they arrived home in San Francisco or at their home airports. As you can imagine, this didn't help their adjustment back to civilian life.

For many Vietnam veterans who were fortunate to return home to their families, their battle wasn't over; they forever carried a hidden enemy within, which left them scarred emotionally. It was a difficult adjustment, as their families can attest to. Their loved ones returned, but they weren't the same people; the war had changed them. They didn't want to talk about their Vietnam experience. Many weren't able to make the adjustment and led difficult lives, coping through alcohol or drug dependency, trouble holding jobs, failed marriages, etc.

These dedicated men and women sacrificed so much, with some giving their lives and others losing limbs to protect our individual freedoms. The ones who were lucky enough to return home suffered from a manner of illnesses, some physical but mostly mental. They were tortured every day by the things they saw and had to deal with while there. It is something that they never truly got over.

Concerns About Veterans Mental Health, by Daniel Zwerdling, an article published July 24, 2015.

A new study of veterans from the Vietnam War has troubling implications for troops who have fought much more recently in Afghanistan and Iraq. The study suggests that while it's been 40 years since the Vietnam War ended, hundreds of thousands of those vets still struggle every day with mental health problems linked to their war experiences.

ZWERLING: Congress has ordered these studies to find out how war affects soldiers over their whole lives. Charles Marmar led the latest look at almost 2000 vets. He's chairman of the psychiatry department at the NYU medical school. He says, first, let's focus on the encouraging findings. Seventy to seventy-five percent of the Vietnam vets they studied have never suffered mental illness linked to war. They did not get PTSD or depression. They did not become alcoholics or drug addicts.

MARMAR: It doesn't mean they haven't been affected by their experiences for sure. To go to war is a profound experience. It changes you forever in many ways. But they didn't break down with a psychiatric illness.

ZWERDLING: The study is officially called the National Vietnam Veterans Longitudinal Study. And, now, here's the sobering finding. Roughly 11 percent of the vets they studied are in serious trouble. They still suffer from PTSD or disorders like it, and that's around 20 times the rate among veterans who did not serve in Vietnam. The Vietnam vets still get flashbacks. They're irritable and depressed. They can't sleep well.

MARMAR: A number of them are quite alienated from their family and friends and have trouble either in the workplace or in their family environments, those kinds of troubles.

ZWERDLING: Marmar says when you extrapolate those findings, it suggests that more than a quarter of a million Vietnam vets still struggle every day. And Judith Broder says those findings should make you worry about what's going to happen with the troops who fought in Iraq and Afghanistan. Broder is also a psychiatrist. She founded the Soldiers Project in California. They've given mental health counseling to hundreds of young troops and family members. She says every vet in trouble affects at least ten relatives and friends.

ZWERDLING: The Vietnam veterans' study was published in the latest issue of the Journal of the American Medical Association Psychiatry. Daniel Zwerdling, NPR News. Transcript provided by NPR, Copyright NPR.

Comments from interviewing Gene and Loa Dawn Vincent: Gene and Loa Dawn said, "Steve was a changed person when he returned. He was edgy and unsettled and began to drink a lot. He couldn't sleep in a bed, often sleeping on a couch or even on the floor with his Army blanket over him." More than likely a result of spending 265 days straight without a bed in Vietnam, sleeping in a tent or foxhole. Over the years, he took odd farm jobs and finally found a level of peace and happiness when he purchased a farm on his own, raising cattle and lending a hand to the family with the help of his loyal dog, Duke."

Comments from interviewing Frank "Hazel" Farrell: Frank said, "When I returned to California, the protesters were not happy to see us. They threw tomatoes, apples, and other junk at us, and called us "baby killers."

From the book Walking Point, A Vietnam Memoir by Robert Kunkel

I can only speak for myself, but I believe the war, in a major dimension, changed everyone who fought in it. Death knocked at your door every day, at least in your own mind. On some days, the reality of death came within inches or even a fraction of an inch. It destroyed some lives physically and mentally. It also built friendships that would last a lifetime. For many, the physical scars are souvenirs. Psychological scars are ingrained in brain cells for eternity.

When recounting a war-related incident, there was a tendency to laugh about it. Frequently the laugh is a smokescreen to keep from crying. Some stories you just don't talk about. These are the events that pry into your mind, keeping you awake at night and forever vigilant. The battles of Vietnam are over, but the battle in the mind never ends.

In our family, it seems like everyone talks, and no one listens. After the hellos, there were hundreds of questions shot at me. After answering a few, I clammed up. My younger sister asked, "What's it like to kill someone?" I turned and walked out of the house. Our family farmhouse sat just 150 yards from the shore of Pearl Lake. I walked down to the lake and strolled along the shore. I was thinking to myself; this was going to take some getting used to. I didn't know what was going on inside me, but I couldn't take all this attention.

The night wound down. Those who needed to leave left. Mom saw to it that I had the same bed as when I left home. I crawled into bed and lay there for an hour. Once I was sure everyone was asleep, I got up, got dressed, and went outside. I walked behind the house and sat up against a large elm tree on the lawn. I sat there for a long time before I dozed off. I slept for two hours. After waking, I took a walk down to the lake again and listened to the lap of the water in the dark. It was a pleasant sound. I had never noticed that before.

While I was home, I had a difficult time adjusting to this home life. Almost every night, I waited for the rest of the family to fall asleep, and then I would get up and take a walk in the night. When I felt I needed to sleep, I picked the large elm tree and sat up against this. The base of the tree protruded out in two spots and formed a flat area where I could lean and it was very comfortable for me. Every morning I would quietly sneak back into the house and go to my bed and be there when the wake-up call came.

The home lifestyle was too laid back and mundane. I became bored easily. If I could have admitted it, I was actually missing Vietnam. I was missing the friends I had made there, but I was also missing the sounds of artillery, helicopters, and planes. It was too quiet here.

Comments from interviewing Gene and Loa Dawn Vincent: "Gene and Loa Dawn said, "Steve returned home and had trouble adjusting based on what he went through in Vietnam. There was one instance where he was helping to harvest in the fall, driving a tractor with a corn picker, and pulling a wagon. Although Steve knew a family member was riding in the wagon and planning to shoot pheasants, when the shot rang out, he basically went into flashback mode and broke down. It took him quite a while to recover, and I think we were all more aware of our actions after that."

Comments from interviewing Jerry "Nick" Nicholson's sister Dorothy: Dorothy said, "My brother Jerry and other servicemen arrived at the local airport at 5 AM, and protesters threw eggs and cursed at them." Dorothy added, "My brother Jerry and ex-husband really had a difficult time adjusting to civilian life after they returned from Vietnam." They resorted to alcohol and appeared to be angry at the world." She added, "Jerry eventually was able to adjust and settled down with a good job and raised a family." I think this was due to Jerry's faith and our close family support. However, she said, "My ex-husband never fully adjusted, and when he returned, there wasn't group counseling, etc., to help with his adjustment."

Comments from Interviewing Steve Streeter: Steve said, "I remember when we returned to stateside and landed in California, we were shocked when we got off the plane. No welcome home parties. It was just the opposite with adults and even little kids throwing rocks at us and calling us names." Steve added, "I really had a tough adjustment and turned to alcohol to cope with my feelings. Unlike some who were never able to adjust, over time, I was able to move on with my life because of the love and strength of my wife, Georgia."

Article featuring Veteran Sarah Blum, a decorated Vietnam Veteran, Author. From The High Ground Newsletter, June 2022, thehighground.us.

I left Vietnam, where I came in, from Bien Hoa Airbase. There were a couple hundred of us lined up on the tarmac in the 100-degree heat, waiting for what we called the "freedom bird," the plane that would take us home. We all felt like sitting ducks because the airbase was hit with mortars very frequently, especially when soldiers were waiting to leave. I know I wasn't the only one who thought and felt that. When the plane came, it was pink and orange, the color of Southwest Airlines. Everyone was tense until the moment the plane actually lifted off the tarmac. At that point, I could hear everyone taking it in, a much-needed deep breath. It was a loud collective intake of air and relief, "we made it out alive."

I came into Travis AFB and had to try to get to San Francisco International to get a plane to LA. I felt like I was in a fog. They kept us on the plane at Travis for two hours before they let us deplane. They said it was for our safety and told us not to wear our uniforms. They had waited until there were very few people in the airport to let us off. Apparently, uniformed service members were being harassed and attacked by anti-war protestors, so we were cautioned not to be in uniform for our own well-being. My mind could not phantom what I was being told. "You mean I spent a hellish year in amid war, caring for my brother's soldiers' wounds, and now I am home safe, but I am at risk here because of my service."

I took a red and silver bus from Travis AFB to SF International Airport, and it was raining. I remember looking out of the windows of the bus and noting the raindrops on the window and finding myself feeling like I was in the raindrop. The rain seemed friendlier than anything else at that moment.

I was headed to LA to see my nurse friends I worked with before going to Vietnam. It was late at night, and I was so glad finally to have someone who was glad to see me. The next day I had my first experience of culture shock. When I was on the way to the hospital to visit my friend Bea, and an ambulance went by with the siren blaring. I instinctively dove into the foot well of the car as though expecting an attack. My friend Ellie was shocked by my reaction, and so was I. Later, when we went into a supermarket, I stepped on the pad in front of the door, and the door suddenly flew open; I jumped back. It took me a while to acclimate to society.

I stepped into my role as the head nurse of the orthopedic ward to take care of "my brother soldiers." I was glad to be out of the operating room and be able to listen to them and talk to them. I received them when they came back from Vietnam, often through a hospital in Guam or Japan, checking their wounds and letting the doctor know. I got them settled, arranged for a special meal of their choosing, and brought the portable phone to their bedside if they were bedridden so they could talk to family members. I loved my job in 1968 as head nurse of ward six, and I felt great physically, mentally, and emotionally. That was when I first started to understand the impact of the war on my brother's soldiers' bodies, minds, and spirits. Their physical wounds often would not heal quickly enough, and I knew intuitively that it was because their mind and emotions were struggling. That was the beginning of my search to understand what we now know as PTSD.

From 1968-1970 I was a student at Seattle University and was exposed to the Black Panthers and the protests against the war, with me being a target. I stopped telling everyone that I was a nurse who served in Vietnam. In 1970 I married another Vietnam veteran, and we had two children. Twelve years later, I was part of the very first women's veteran's group at the Seattle Vets Center for 16 weeks and then did another 16 weeks after that to deal with my PTSD symptoms. That was not enough, and by 1984 I was doing therapy with a trauma specialist until 1987. From then on, I have worked with veterans and civilians to help them heal their PTSD. Now today, 2021, my book Warrior Nurse: PTSD and Healing, are being considered for publication.

Organizations and communities are starting to honor and recognize our veterans, and it's never too late and is always welcomed for those who served.

Comments from Interviewing Steve Streeter: Steve said, "In 2017, I went on this Honor Flight that left from Ft Dodge, Iowa to Washington D.C. It was amazing from start to finish, even though it only lasted about 24 hours. Everything was paid for from donations. There were over 130 veterans from all kinds of conflicts; WWII, Korea, Vietnam, Iraq, and Afghanistan. We were treated like royalty. When we arrived at Dulles Airport in Virginia, there were over 1500 people that welcomed us. The fire department had hoses spraying across the plane, signifying recognition and honor. They said I would shed a few tears on the trip, and I did, with the first being when we deplaned. It took two hours for all of us to deplane because each individual was saluted at the bottom of the stairs before the next walked down the stairs. A Marine held his salute for the full two hours. We all were overwhelmed. We saw all the amazing sites around D.C., from the Lincoln Memorial to the WWII, Korean, and Vietnam memorials. The next tear-jerker was when we went to Arlington Cemetery and witnessed the changing of the guard. When we returned to Ft Dodge, it was around 3 AM, and over 1000 people greeted us. The trip helped a lot of us heal, which was long overdue."

A "Quilt of Valor" was presented to Steve Streeter in 2022 by Alyson (Toyne) Schroeder. The quilt was a labor of love from the National Quilt of Valor Organization. A Quilt of Valor is awarded to service members and veterans who have been touched by war. It says, thank you for your service and sacrifice in serving our nation. It signifies that communities are continuing to recognize their previously forgotten veterans from the Vietnam War. As of today, over 300,000 quilts have been presented to veterans. Steve's eyes watered when he talked to me about the quilt. It meant the world to him that someone would care and spend so much time and effort to recognize him.

Quilt of Valor, "Home of the Brave and Land of the Free," from Steve Streeter

Today, too often, our current generation takes our freedoms for granted and doesn't understand the sacrifices individuals like Leon and previous generations went through to preserve those freedoms. Once having read the letters and stories in this book, you need to stop and think how lucky we are to have individuals like my brother and his Vietnam buddies and be thankful for them and others who served. We must not forget those who protect our freedoms every day. We are so lucky to live in this great country where the individuals described in this book protect those freedoms. Remember, "Freedom isn't free."

Bibliography

THE GROUND YOU STAND UPON

2019, Co-authored by Joshua Bowe and his dad Wilbur Bowe. Wilbur Bowe was assigned to the mortar platoon of Alpha Company, 5/7th Cav, in Vietnam from August 1966 to August 1967.

1966 THE YEAR OF THE HORSE

2009, by Robert K. Powers – Robert K. Powers was an Indirect Fire Infantryman assigned to the mortar platoon of Bravo Company, 5/7th Cav. He was drafted in January 1966 and sent to Vietnam as an early replacement in October of the same year.

WALKING POINT – A VIETNAM MEMOIR

Written by Robert Kunkel, 1st Air Division, 5th Battalion, 7th Cavalry, Bravo Company in Vietnam 1966-1967.

INTERIM REPORT OF OPERATIONS, 1st Cavalry Division, July 1965 to December 1966

Compiled by Charles S. Sykes, published by 1st Cavalry Division Association

OPERATIONAL REPORT – LESSONS LEARNED, 1st Cavalry Division (Air Mobile), period Ending 31 July 1967

1st Cavalry Division (Air Mobile) Headquarters, Declassified 31 December 1973.

AFTER ACTION REPORT (3 September 66 Attack on Camp Ratcliff)

17 September 1966, 1st Cavalry Division (Air Mobile) Headquarters, Declassified 17 September 1978.

OPERATION THAYER II (Wikipedia)

McGarrigle, George L. (1998). Taking the Offensive: October 1966 to October 1967. Center of Military History,

United States Army. ISBN 9781780394145. This article incorporates text from this source, which is in the public domain.

PRESIDENTIAL UNIT CITATION FOR THE PERIOD 30 SEP 1966 TO 30 SEP 1967, AND ARMY SUPPORTING DOCUMENTATION AND PHOTOS FROM THE NATIONAL ARCHIVES, COLLEGE PARK, MARYLAND

Information for the $5^{TH}/7^{TH}$ Cavalry Division (Air Mobile), obtained from the National Archives, College Park, Maryland.

WHAT IT WAS REALLY LIKE AS A MEDIC IN THE VIETNAM WAR Read More

What I was Like Really Like to be a Medic In Vietnam Read More, https://www.grunge.com/321306/what-it- was-really-like-as-a-medic-in-the-Vietnam-war/?utmcampaign=clip

A HISTORY OF THE 12TH EVAC HOSPITAL, ARTICLE BY STUART M. POTICHA, MD, CAPT. USARMY 1966-1968. Tropical Lightning Flashes Newsletter by the 25th Infantry Division.

Dr. Stuart Poticha was a Capt., and Dr. in the Army in Vietnam at the 12 Evac Hospital. He met Steve Streeter on the trip over on the USNS Patrick, where he diagnosed Steve's burst appendix and operated immediately, and was more than likely was responsible for saving Steve's life.

ARTICLE FEATURING VETERAN SARAH BLUM, A DECORATED VIETNAM VETERAN AND AUTHOR. FROM THE WISCONSIN HIGH GROUND NEWSLETTER, JUNE 2022. THEHIGHGROUND.US

Sarah L. Blum, ARNP, is a decorated Nurse Vietnam Veteran, retired nurse psychotherapist, and Author. Sarah's new book, Warrior Nurse PTSD and Healing, is ready for publication.

SCOUT DOGS IN VIETNAM

"The Dogs of the Vietnam War.", Together we Served Blog. Vietnam War Dogs, November 9, 2013, by Fred Childs, from *Vietnam War Dogs* 1965-1972; https://charliecompany.org/charlie-company-troops/troops-2. It talks about how critical scout dogs were to saving lives and contributing to successful operations.

DOG BECOMES A FIGHTER WHEN THE PRESSURES ON

Dog Becomes a Fighter When the Pressure's On, NEWSPAPER ARCHIVE, Pacific Stars and Stripes, July 22, 1967, p7, Tokyo, Tokyo, JP, https//newspaperarchive.com/pa-stars-and-jul22-1967-p-7/

1st-Cavalry-Division-Airmobile-Bon Song Vietnam-RTO and his CO and "The Most Important Tactical Field Item" in the Vietnam War History Net. HISTORYNET website; www.historynet.com/event/vietnam-war.

CONCERNS ABOUT VETERANS' MENTAL HEALTH, article by Daniel Zwerdling

Concerns About Veterans Mental Health article was published on July 24, 2015, by Daniel Zwerdling. It is a summary of the National Vietnam Veterans Longitudinal Study published in the Journal of American Medical Association Psychiatry.

Glossary

Agent Orange: An herbicide and defoliant chemical sprayed in large quantities over the jungle areas of South Vietnam in total concealment to guerrilla forces.

Air Mobile: Soldiers who jump out of helicopters.

APO: Army Post Office. Used for mailing purposes.

ARVN: Army of the Republic of Vietnam. Friendly Army military during the Vietnam War.

AWOL: Away Without Leave, unauthorized absence from your duty location.

Base Camp: Large military installation with some permanent structures and airfields, surrounded by perimeter wire and guard towers.

CH-47: Boeing Chinook large twin-propeller helicopter used as a troop transport, air assault, and supply.

Charlie. Viet Cong.

CO: Commanding officer: Officer in command of your unit.

Commo wire: Two-strand coated wire used for land communication.

Company: 175 men, typically four platoons.

CP: Command Post: Main command and control leadership center for military operations.

CPA: Command Post Alternate: Military additional command post in the field.

C-rations: Canned military food rations distributed to soldiers in the field.

Dustoff: A medical evacuation operation. Dustoff in Vietnam was a crew of four dedicated men that flew unarmed helicopters to the front line and beyond to rescue wounded soldiers.

ETS: Estimated Time of Separation. The date military personnel tour of duty is up.

Gunship: Heavily armed HU-1B helicopter for Infantry support.

Hooch: A single-family dwelling.

Huey: Bell UH-1 Iroquois, the helicopter used for troop transport, air assault, supply, and gunship.

KIA: Killed in action.

KP: Kitchen Police. Military personnel assigned to work kitchen duty.

LP: Long Range Patrol. Term for Army troops on an extended mission patrolling outside their camp/base.

LZ: Landing Zone. Military operations are where you set up temporary operations.

Massif: A large mass or compact group of connected mountains forming an independent portion of a range.

Medevac: Evacuation of wounded by helicopter.

Medic: Army MOS duties include prepping wounded soldiers for triage and evacuation. Administering IVs and taking vital signs, and dressing and sterilizing wounds.

MOS: Military Operations Specialty. Your designated military job.

Mule: One-seat motorized cart used for light loads for a short distance.

M-16: Standard rife issued to soldiers in Vietnam, beginning in 1965, replacing the M-14.

OP: Operational Patrol. The term is used for Army troops patrolling near their military camp/base.

PAVN/VC: People's Army Vietnam/Vietcong. Enemy Army military during the Vietnam War.

PE: Post Exchange. Army facility where you can purchase supplies, etc.

PFC: Private First Class. The second enlisted Army military rank.

Platoon: forty-four men, 4 squads.

PLC: Patrol Leader Council. A clerk who supports unit requirements.

PRC-25: Principal infantry radio was used in Vietnam.

R&R: Rest and Recuperation. A term used when you're authorized to be away from the combat area.

RL-31: Army term for a roll of Commo wire spooled around an axle.

RTO: Army MOS, Radio Telephone Operator. Military term for a telephone operator. Duties include being responsible for reporting conflicts or firefights to headquarters, which would, in turn, provide support, whether air or ground, to units that were in conflict.

SP/4: Army rank of Specialist Fourth Class. The fourth enlisted rank, two chevrons, and three bars.

TET: The TET offensive. An operation launched by the PAVN and the Viet Cong against the US and South Vietnamese military.

TT: Target Tracking. Prioritized radio traffic for tracking military operations.

Wireman: Army MOS includes the installation of telephones and switchboards and laying wire and cable. Tactical Switching Operators and Field Wiremen adjust equipment for proper operation. They recover wire, locate wire system faults, and operate switchboards.

XO. Executive Officer, second in command.

101: A type of Army ration.

5th Bn/ 7th Cal, HHQ: Army organization of 5th Battalion, 7th Cavalry, Higher Headquarters Squadron.

www.ingramcontent.com/pod-product-compliance
Lightning Source LLC
Chambersburg PA
CBHW070152100426
42743CB00013B/2890